KU-675-360

ntents

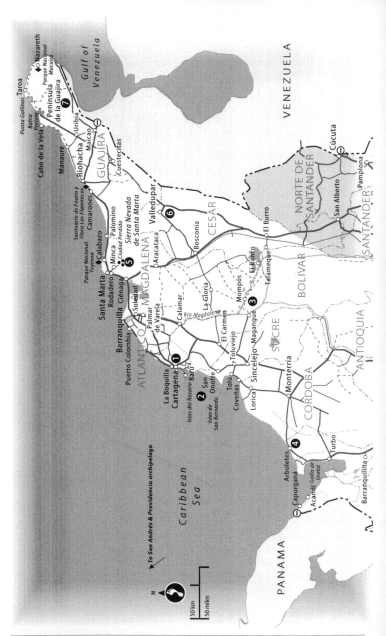

Reaching the lowlands of Colombia's Caribbean coast is like entering another world. Steamy, colourful and lively, the entire area pulses to the rhythms of the omnipresent *vallenato*. *Costeños* may be looked down on by their more sombre countrymen, intimating that they lack the same sophistication and work ethic, but they certainly know how to enjoy themselves. There are almost endless fiestas, including the Baranquilla Carnival, which is often cited as second only to Rio for colour and size and it's also much less commercial.

Dancing and drinking aside, there is fine architecture and an impressive literary legacy, particularly in Cartagena, the emerald in the crown of Colombia. This stunning colonial city is positively bursting with colour and history, and offers fine food, a lively nightlife and various sparkling coral islands within easy reach.

South from Cartagena is Mompós, a colonial town where the clocks seem to have stopped back in the early 20th century. Its main claim to fame is one of the best Easter festivals in the world. Up the Gulf of Urabá, on the way to Panama, are the villages of Acandí, Capurganá and Sapzurro, unreachable by road and with a wild shoreline of coral reefs and the virgin jungles of the Darién.

Travel east along the coast and you'll reach Santa Marta, Colombia's oldest city and gateway to the spectacular Tayrona National Park. Rising up from the shores is the Sierra Nevada de Santa Marta, the highest coastal mountain range in the world, and one of the few places that can boast tropical beaches and snow-capped mountains within 20 miles. The Sierra Nevada was home to the Tayrona culture and the trek to Ciudad Perdida must come high on anyone's list of Latin American adventures. On the inland side of the mountain range is Valledupar, the birthplace of *vallenato* and a good place to find out about the sierra's indigenous peoples.

Beyond Santa Marta is the arid landscape of the Guajira Peninsula, home to the indigenous Wayúu, enormous flocks of flamingos and the ethereal Cabo de la Vela, where turquoise waters lap against a desert shoreline.

Planning your trip

Where to go in Cartagena and the Caribbean Coast

Cartagena is colonial Spain's finest legacy in the Americas, impressive in every respect. Beyond the historic centre is a big modern city, with many of the problems inherent in urban communities. Spend several days here as there is so much to see. It is also the best base for visits to the Caribbean coast and the nearby islands: check out the beaches, the watersports and the strange mud volcanoes nearby. Cartagena is also the gateway to San Andrés, a popular island resort, and to the charming neighbouring island of Providencia. To the northeast, Barranquilla has its own attractions, including a spectacular carnival, perhaps the finest in Latin America after Rio de Janeiro. Northeast of Barranquilla is Santa Marta, currently undergoing a facelift to its colonial quarter and welcoming increasing numbers of tourists who explore the Tayrona National Park, the Sierra Nevada de Santa Marta and the beautiful beaches beyond. The remote Guajira Peninsula is an adventurous trip to the cultures and wildlife of the semi-desert at the extreme northeast of the Colombia's Caribbean coast. By contrast, the southwest corner, which adjoins Panama, is an adventure of a different kind: boats will take you to villages with tropical beaches, sheltering beneath the forests of Darién. Mompós is a superb colonial town that can be visited from Cartagena or other points in the region, but its relative isolation means that you will have to stay at least one night. The other important inland city in the region is Valledupar, whose influence, in the form of *vallenato* music is heard on every street throughout the Caribbean. As well as the culture, Valledupar is worth a visit in its own right for the access it gives to the Sierra Nevada de Santa Marta.

Best time to visit Cartagena and the Caribbean Coast

Being so close to the equator, the climate varies little in Colombia and you will see plenty of sun year-round. There are no seasons to speak of and temperatures are dictated mainly by altitude. The best time for a visit is December to February, on average the driest months. It's worth remembering, though, that this is holiday season for many Colombians and prices rise significantly in the most popular places, and transport, including domestic flights, can be busy. During this period, a number of major annual fiestas are held, for example **Barranquilla Carnival** in February. Equally, Easter is a local holiday time and almost every town has superb celebrations, Mompós chief among them. In July and August, accommodation prices tend to rise because of school holidays.

Getting to Cartagena and the Caribbean Coast

Air
Most international fights arrive at Bogotá from where there are onward connections to Cartagena (see page 25 for airport information), Barranquilla and San Andrés with several of the airlines listed below. International fights direct to Cartagena go from Fort Lauderdale (**Spirit**), Miami (**Avianca**), New York (**Jet Blue**) and Panama (**Copa**). There are also international fights to Barranquilla from Miami (**Avianca**) and Panama (**Copa**). Fares are signifcantly cheaper outside the peaks times of Easter, July, August and December to mid-January.

From Europe There are flights to Bogotá with **Avianca** from Barcelona and Madrid (also **Iberia** from Madrid), **Air France** from Paris and **Lufthansa** from Frankfurt.

From North America Avianca flies from several North American cities: New York, Miami, Fort Lauderdale, Orlando and Washington. Other carriers from North America are **American** (Miami), **Delta** (Atlanta, New York), **United** (Houston, Newark), **Jet Blue** (Fort Lauderdale, Orlando), **Spirit** (Fort Lauderdale) and **Air Canada** (Toronto).

From Latin America Bogotá can also be reached from many Latin American and Caribbean cities with **Avianca, LAN, Copa, Tame, AeroGal, Conviasa** and **AeroMéxico**.

Road
To get to Cartagena from neighbouring countries overland, the only possibility is by road from Venezuela. It is not possible to enter Colombia from Panama by road.

Sea
There are few options for arriving in Cartagena by sea. These are limited to cruise ships, tourist boats sailing between Panama and Cartagena (see page 43) and local pleasure trips.

Transport in Cartagena and the Caribbean Coast

Air
Avianca ① www.avianca.com, is the national carrier. Other airlines are **LAN Colombia** ① www.lan.com; **Copa Airlines Colombia** ① www.copaair.com; **Satena** ① www.satena.com, government owned but linked with Avianca on some flights; **EasyFly** ① www.easyfly. com.co, a budget airline serving Bogotá, Medellín, Cartagena and other smaller cities; **Viva Colombia** ① www.vivacolombia.co, a budget airline serving Barranquilla, Bogotá, Cartagena, Medellín, Montería, San Andrés and Santa Marta; and **Aerolínea de Antioquia, ADA** ① www.ada-aero.com, based in Medellín, 19- to 32-seater planes serving most of the country. Domestic airports vary in the services they offer and tourist facilities tend to close early on weekdays, and all day Sunday. Local airport taxes are included in the price. Security checks can be thorough; watch your luggage.

A useful search engine for sourcing cheap flights is **www.despegar.com**. It may be worth using a travel agent to look for flights as they often have discount arrangements with certain airlines. You cannot buy tickets with an international credit card online, but you can pay over the phone. You can check online for good last-minute deals, as well as advance purchase fares.

Road
Almost all the main routes are paved, but the state of the roads, usually single-lane, varies considerably between departments. Journeys are generally comfortable, although heavy traffic can cause delays and landslides frequently close roads after rains.

Bus On the main routes, the bus network is comprehensive and buses are generally efficient. At large bus stations, the choice of carriers can be daunting but the advantage is that services are frequent. The scenery is worth seeing so travel by day if possible; it is also safer and you can keep a better eye on your valuables.

On main routes there is usually a choice of company and type of bus. The cheapest, *corriente*, are local buses, which are uncomfortable and slow, with frequent stops, but offer plenty of local colour. Try to keep your luggage with you. *Pullman* (each company has a different name for the service) are long-distance buses usually with air conditioning, toilets, hostess service and DVDs (almost always violent films, dubbed into Spanish). It's best to sit near the back where it's quieter and you don't have to keep the blinds down. The main companies operating in the region include: **Berlinas del Fonce** ① *www.berlinasdelfonce.com*, **Copetran** ① *www.copetran.com.co*, and **Expreso Brasilia** ① *www.expresobrasilia.com*. *Velotax* and other *busetas* are slightly quicker and more expensive than ordinary buses. They may be called *colectivos*, or *vans* and are usually 12- to 20-seat vehicles, sometimes seven-seater cars or pick-up trucks. It is also possible to order a *puerta-a-puerta* (door-to-door) service at a reasonable price. When taxis provide this service they are *por puestos* (pay by seat) and do not leave till full. Fares shown in the text are no more than a guide. Note that meal stops can be few and far between, and short; it's best to take your own food. Luggage is normally carried in a locked compartment. **If you entrust your luggage to the bus companies' luggage rooms, remember to load it on to the bus yourself; it will not be done automatically.** There are few interdepartmental bus services on public holidays. During holidays and in high season, arrive at the bus terminal at least an hour before the departure time to guarantee a seat, even if you have bought a ticket in advance. If you are joining a bus at popular or holiday times, not at the starting point, you may be left behind even though you have a ticket and reservation. Always take your passport (or photocopy) with you: identity and luggage checks on buses do occur.

Car With a good road network, self-driving is becoming an increasingly popular way of seeing Colombia. The kind of motoring you do will depend on the car you set out with. While a normal car will reach most places of interest, high ground clearance is useful for badly surfaced or unsurfaced roads and for fording rivers. Four-wheel drive vehicles are recommended for flexibility. Wherever you travel you should expect from time to time to find roads that are badly maintained, damaged or closed during the wet season; expect delays because of floods and landslides. There is also the possibility of delays due to major roadworks. Do not plan your schedule too tightly. There are *peajes* (toll stations) every 60-100 km or so on major roads: tolls depend on distance and type of vehicle, but vary from US$2-5.25. Motorcycles and bicycles don't have to pay.

Safety Before taking a long journey, ask locally about the state of the road and check if there are any safety issues. Roads are not always signposted. Avoid night journeys; the roads may not be in good condition, lorry and bus drivers tend to be reckless, and animals often stray onto the roads. Police and military checks can be frequent in troubled areas, keep your documents handy. In town, try to leave your car in an attended *parqueadero* (car park), especially at night. Only park in the street if there is someone on guard, tip US$0.50. Spare no ingenuity in making your car impenetrable. Your model should be like an armoured van: anything less secure can be broken into by the determined and skilled thief. Be sure to note down key numbers and carry spares of the most important ones.

Documents International driving licences are advised, especially if you have your own car. To be accepted, a national driving licence must be accompanied by an official translation if the original is in a language other than Spanish. To bring a car into Colombia, you must also have documents proving ownership of the vehicle, and a tourist card/transit visa. These are normally valid for 90 days and must be applied for at the Colombian consulate in the country which you will be leaving. A *carnet de passages* is recommended when entering with a European registered vehicle. Only third-party insurance issued by a Colombian company is valid; there are agencies in all ports. You will frequently be asked for this document while driving. Carry driving documents with you at all times.

Fuel 'Corriente' 84 octane, US$5 per gallon. More expensive 'Premium 95' octane is only available in large cities. Diesel US$4.55.

Car hire Car hire, though relatively expensive, especially if you are going to the more remote areas and need 4WD or specialist vehicles, is convenient for touring, and the better hotels all have safe parking. The main international car rental companies are represented at principal airports but may be closed on Saturday afternoons and Sundays. There are also local firms in most of the departmental capitals. In addition to a passport and driver's licence, a credit card may be asked for as additional proof of identity and to secure a returnable deposit to cover any liability not covered by the insurance. If renting a Colombian car, note that major cities have the *pico y placa* system, www.picoyplaca.info, which means cars are not allowed to enter the city during morning and afternoon rush hour depending on the day and car number plate (this does not apply at weekends and on public holidays).

Where to stay in Cartagena and the Caribbean Coast

Colombia has a number of quite exceptional hotels that are well worth seeking out. They are usually in colonial towns and not necessarily very expensive. There is a small network of youth hostels, of varying quality and used extensively by Colombian groups, but international members are welcome (see below). Increasingly more budget accommodation and backpacker hostels are opening up, as well as many chic boutique hotels, often in restored colonial buildings.

In peak season (15 December to mid- to late January; 15 June to 31 August) and bank holidays (*puentes*), some hotels in main holiday centres may increase prices by as much as 50%.

The Colombian hotel federation, **COTELCO** ⓘ *www.cotelco.org*, has lists of authorized prices for member hotels, which can be consulted at tourist offices. In theory, all hotels should be registered, but this is not always the case, particularly with cheaper hotels. Most hotels in Colombia charge for extra beds for children, up to a maximum (usually) of four beds per room. Prices are normally displayed at reception, but in quiet periods it is always worth negotiating. Ask to see the room before committing.

When booking a hotel from an airport or bus station, try to speak to the hotel yourself; most will understand at least simple English and possibly French, German or Italian. If you

Price codes

Where to stay

$$$$ over US$150	$$$ US$66-150
$$ US$30-65	$ under US$30

Price of a double room in high season, including taxes.

Restaurants

$$$ over US$12	$$ US$7-12	$ US$6 and under

Prices for a two-course meal for one person, excluding drinks or service charge.

use an official tourist agent you will probably pay a little more as a booking fee. If you accept help from anyone else, you could be putting yourself at risk.

Motels are almost always pay-by-the-hour 'love hotels' for use by illicit lovers, couples still living with their parents, or prostitutes and their clients. Most of the time, especially with the more expensive drive-in ones on the outskirts of town, the names will provide an obvious enough clue (eg 'Passion Motel'), but this is not always the case.

In cheaper hotels, beware of electric shower heaters, which can be dangerous through faulty wiring.

Toilets may suffer from inadequate water supplies. In all cases, however, do not flush paper down the toilet bowl but use the receptacle provided. Carry toilet paper with you as cheaper establishments as well as restaurants, bars, etc may not provide it, or make an additional charge for it.

Camping

Local tourist authorities have lists of official campsites, but they are seldom signposted on main roads, so can be hard to find. Permission to camp with a tent, campervan or car may be granted by landowners in less populated areas. Many *haciendas* have armed guards protecting their property, which can add to your safety. Do not camp on private land without permission. Those in campervans can camp by the roadside, but it is not particularly safe and it can be difficult to find a secluded spot. If you have a vehicle, it is possible to camp at truck drivers' restaurants or sometimes at police or army posts. Check very carefully before deciding to camp: you may be exposing yourself to significant danger. Some hostels, particularly in rural areas, also offer camping and often provide tents and other equipment at an additional cost, but are still cheaper than dorm beds.

Homestays

In many places, it is possible to stay with a local family; check with the local tourist office to see what is available. This is a good option for those interested in learning Spanish informally in a family environment. However, if you take formal classes, you should have a student visa (see Visas and immigration, page 20).

Youth hostels

La Federación Colombiana de Albergues Juveniles (FCAJ) ① *Cra 7, No 6-10, Bogotá, T280 3041, hostelling@fcaj.org.co*. The FCAJ is affiliated to **Hostelling International** ① *www. hihostels.com*. **Colombian Hostels** ① *www.colombianhostels.com.co*, has a good network of 41 members around the country. **Hostel Trail Latin America** ① *Cra 11, No 4-16, Popayán,*

T831 7871, www.hosteltrail.com, is an online network of hostels and tour companies in South America providing information on locally run businesses for backpackers and independent travellers.

Food and drink in Cartagena and the Caribbean Coast

Colombia has yet to reach international renown for its cuisine, but food is becoming more of a draw. Even though you can now find most regional specialities available in all the major cities, there are many local variations to sample in different parts of Colombia.

Some of the standard items on the menu are: *sancocho*, a meat stock (may be fish on the coast) with potato, corn (on the cob), yucca, sweet potato and plantain. *Arroz con pollo* (chicken and rice), one of the standard Latin American dishes, is excellent in Colombia. *Carne asada* (grilled beefsteak), usually an inexpensive cut, is served with *papas fritas* (chips) or rice and you can ask for a vegetable of the day. *Sobrebarriga* (belly of beef) is served with varieties of potato in a tomato and onion sauce. *Huevos pericos* (eggs scrambled with onions and tomatoes) are a popular, cheap and nourishing snack available almost anywhere, especially favoured for breakfast. *Tamales* are meat pies made by folding a maize dough round chopped pork mixed with potato, rice, peas, onions and eggs wrapped in banana leaves (which you don't eat) and steamed. Other ingredients may be added such as olives, garlic, cloves and paprika. Colombians eat *tamales* for breakfast with hot chocolate. *Empanadas* are another popular snack; these are made with chicken or various other meats, or vegetarian filling, inside a maize dough and deep fried in oil. *Patacones* are cakes of mashed and baked *platano* (large green banana). *Arepas* are standard throughout Colombia; these are flat maize griddle cakes often served instead of bread or as an alternative. *Pan de bono* is cheese flavoured bread. *Almojábanas*, a kind of sour milk/cheese bread roll, are great for breakfast when freshly made. *Buñuelos* are 4- to 6-cm balls of wheat flour and eggs mixed and deep-fried, also best when still warm. *Arequipe* is a sugar-based brown syrup used with desserts and in confectionary, universally savoured by Colombians. *Brevas* (figs) with *arequipe* are one of the most popular desserts.

Regional specialities
Fish is naturally a speciality in the coastal regions. In *Arroz con coco* the rice is prepared with coconut. *Cazuela de mariscos*, a soup/stew of shellfish and white fish, maybe including octopus and squid, is especially good. *Sancocho de pescado* is a fish stew with vegetables, usually simpler and cheaper than *cazuela*. *Chipichipi*, a small clam found along the coast in Barranquilla and Santa Marta, is a standard local dish served with rice. *Empanada* (or *arepa*) *de huevo*, is deep fried with eggs in the middle and is a good light meal. *Canasta de coco* is a good local sweet: pastry containing coconut custard flavoured with wine and surmounted by meringue.

Restaurants
In Cartagena you will find a limitless choice of menu and price. Other large towns have a good range of specialist restaurants and all the usual fast-food outlets, Colombian and international. In the smaller towns and villages not catering for tourists, you'll find a modest selection of places to eat. Be sure to check opening times for the evenings, particularly at weekends; some places may close around 1800. On Sundays it can be particularly difficult to eat in a restaurant and even hotel restaurants may be closed.

Most of the bigger cities have specific vegetarian restaurants and you will find them listed in the text. They are normally open only for lunch. In towns and villages you will have to ask for special food to be prepared.

The main Colombian meal of the day is at lunchtime, the *almuerzo* or *menú ejecutivo/del día*, with soup, main course and fruit juice or *gaseosa* (soft drink). If you are economizing, ask for the *plato del día*, *bandeja* or *plato corriente* (just the main dish). This can be found everywhere and restaurants usually display the menu and cost in the window or on a board.

The cheapest food can be found in markets (when they are open), from street stalls in downtown areas and at transport terminals, but bear in mind it might not be safe or agree with you. The general rules apply: keep away from uncooked food and salads, and eat fruit you have peeled yourself. Watch what the locals are eating as a guide to the best choice. Having said that, take it easy with dishes that are unfamiliar especially if you have arrived from a different climate or altitude. Wash it down with something out of a sealed bottle. If you find the fresh fruit drinks irresistible, you will have to take your chances! ▸▸ *See Health, page 15.*

Drinks

Colombian coffee is always mild. *Tinto*, the national small cup of black coffee, is taken at all hours. The name is misleading; don't expect to get a glass of red. If you want it strong, ask for *café cargado*; a *tinto doble* is a large cup of black coffee. Coffee with milk is called *café perico*; *café con leche* is a mug of milk with coffee added. If you want a coffee with less milk, order *tinto y leche aparte* and they will bring the milk separately.

Tea is popular but herbal rather than Indian or Chinese: ask for *(bebida) aromática*; flavours include *limonaria*, *orquídea* and *manzanilla*. If you want Indian tea, *té Lipton en agua* should do the trick. *Té de menta* (mint tea) is another of many varieties available but you may have to go to an upmarket café or *casa de té*, which can be found in all of the bigger cities. Chocolate is also drunk: *chocolate Santafereño* is often taken during the afternoon with snacks and cheese. *Agua de panela* (hot water with unrefined sugar) is a common beverage, also made with limes, milk or cheese.

Bottled soft drinks are universal and standard, commonly called *gaseosas*. If you want non-carbonated, ask for *sin gas*. Again you will find that many fruits are used for bottled drinks. Water comes in bottles, cartons and small plastic packets, or even plastic bags: all safer than out of the tap, although tap water is generally of a reasonable quality.

Many acceptable brands of beer are produced, until recently almost all produced by the Bavaria group. Each region has a preference for different brands. The most popular are **Aguila**, **Club Colombia**, **Costeña** and **Poker**.

A traditional drink in Colombia is *chicha*. It is corn-based but sugar and/or *panela* are added and it is boiled. It is served as a non-alcoholic beverage, but if allowed to ferment over several days, and especially if kept in the fridge for a while, it becomes very potent.

The local rum is good and cheap; ask for *ron*, not *aguardiente*. One of the best rums is **Ron Viejo de Caldas**, another (dark) is **Ron Medellín**. Try *canelazo* cold or hot rum with water, sugar, lime and cinnamon. As common as rum is *aguardiente* (literally 'fire water'), a white spirit distilled from sugar cane. There are two types, with *anís* (aniseed) or without. Local table wines include **Isabella**; none is very good. Wine is very expensive: as much as US$15 in restaurants for an acceptable bottle of Chilean or Argentine wine, more for European and other wines.

Fruit and juices

Colombia has an exceptional range and quality of fruit – another aspect of the diversity of altitude and climate. Fruits familiar in northern and Mediterranean climates, though with some differences, include: *manzanas* (apples); *bananos* (bananas); *uvas* (grapes); *limones* (limes; lemons, the larger yellow variety, are rarely seen); *mangos* (mangoes); *melones* (melons); *naranjas* (oranges; usually green or yellow in Colombia); *duraznos* (peaches); and *peras* (pears).

Then there are the local fruits: *chirimoyas* (a green fruit, white inside with pips); *curuba* (banana passion fruit); *feijoa* (a green fruit with white flesh, high in vitamin C); *guayaba* (guava); *guanábana* (soursop); *lulo* (a small orange fruit); *maracuyá* (passion fruit); *mora* (literally 'black berry' but dark red more like a loganberry); *papaya*; the delicious *pitahaya* (taken either as an appetizer or dessert); *sandía* (watermelon); *tomate de árbol* (tree tomato, several varieties normally used as a fruit); and many more.

All of these fruits can be served as juices, either with milk (hopefully fresh) or water (hopefully bottled or sterilized). Most hotels and restaurants are careful about this and you can watch the drinks being prepared on street stalls. Fruit yoghurts are nourishing and cheap; **Alpina** brand is good; *crema* style is best. Also, **Kumis** is a type of liquid yoghurt. Another drink you must try is *champús*, a corn base with fruit, *panela*, cloves and cinnamon added.

Festivals in Cartagena and the Caribbean Coast

García Márquez once said, "five Colombians in a room invariably turns into a party". It could also be said that a couple of hundred Colombians in a village invariably turns into a fiesta. Colombians will use almost anything as a pretext for a celebration. Every city, town and village has at least three or four annual events in which local products and traditions are celebrated with music, dancing and raucous revelry (these are listed throughout the book). Below are some of the most significant. ▸▸ *See also Public holidays, page 17.*

January
End Jan Hay Festival Cartagena, www.hayfestival.com/cartagena. A branch of the UK's Hay Festival turns Cartagena into a focus for all things literary for 4 days.

February
End Jan/early Feb Fiestas de Nuestra Señora de la Candelaria. Celebrated in towns, including Cartagena, this religious cult festival was inherited from the Canary Islands, where 2 goat herders witnessed the apparition of the Virgin Mary holding a green candle.

February-March
Barranquilla Carnival (movable), www.carnavaldebarranquilla.org. Beginning 4 days before Ash Wed, this is one of the best carnivals in South America.

4 days of partying are compulsory by law and involve parades and plenty of dancing.
End Feb or early Mar Cartagena International Film Festival, www.ficci festival.com. One of South America's most important festivals of cinema.

March-April
Semana Santa (Holy Week) (movable). Celebrated all over Colombia, but the processions in Mompós are particularly revered.

April
26-30 Apr Festival de la Leyenda Vallenata, www.festivalvallenato.com. One of the most important music festivals in Colombia, 4 days of music making, celebrations and serious competition in Valledupar culminate in the selection

of the best *vallenato* song and musicians in various categories.

November

First 2 weeks of Nov Independence of Cartagena and Concurso Nacional de la Belleza. Cartagena celebrates being the first department to win Independence from the Spanish each 11 Nov with parades and traditional dancing in the streets. This has been somewhat supplanted by the National Beauty Pageant in which the winner will go on to represent Colombia at Miss Universe.

Essentials A-Z

Accident and emergency

General line for all emergencies: T123;
Fire: T119; **Red Cross emergency**: T132;
CAI Police: T156. If you have problems
with theft or other forms of crime, contact
a **Centro de Atención Inmediata (CAI)**
office for assistance. Make sure you obtain
police/medical reports in order to file
insurance claims.

Electricity

110 Volts AC, alternating at 60 cycles
per second. Most sockets accept both
continental European (round) and
North American (flat) 2-pin plugs.

Embassies and consulates

For embassies and consulates of Colombia,
see http://embassy.goabroad.com.

Health

See your GP or travel clinic at least 6 weeks
before departure for general advice on
travel risks and vaccinations. Try phoning
a specialist travel clinic if your own doctor
is unfamiliar with health conditions in
Colombia. Make sure you have sufficient
medical travel insurance, get a dental check,
know your own blood group and if you
suffer a long-term condition such as diabetes
or epilepsy, obtain a Medic Alert bracelet/
necklace (www.medicalert.co.uk). If you wear
glasses, take a copy of your prescription.

Vaccinations

It is advisable to vaccinate against polio,
tetanus, diphtheria, typhoid, hepatitis A, and
also rabies if going to more remote areas.

Health risks

The most common cause of travellers'
diarrhoea is from eating contaminated
food. In Colombia, drinking water is rarely
the culprit, although it's best to be cautious
(see below). Swimming in sea or river water
that has been contaminated by sewage
can also be a cause; ask locally if it is safe.
Diarrhoea may be also caused by viruses,
bacteria (such as E-coli), protozoal (such
as giardia), salmonella and cholera. It may
be accompanied by vomiting or by severe
abdominal pain. Any kind of diarrhoea
responds well to the replacement of water
and salts. Sachets of rehydration salts can
be bought in most chemists and can be
dissolved in boiled water. If the symptoms
persist, consult a doctor. Tap water in the
major cities is in theory safe to drink but
it may be advisable to err on the side of
caution and drink only bottled or boiled
water. Avoid having ice in drinks unless
you trust that it is from a reliable source.

Mosquitoes are more of a nuisance
than a serious hazard but some, of course,
are carriers of serious diseases such as
malaria, so it is sensible to avoid being
bitten as much as possible. Sleep off the
ground and use a mosquito net and some
kind of insecticide. Mosquito coils release
insecticide as they burn and are available
in many shops, as are tablets of insecticide,
which are placed on a heated mat plugged
into a wall socket.

Money → US$1 = 1934 pesos; UK£1 =3008 pesos; €1=2554 pesos (Oct 2013).

Colombia's currency is the peso. New
coins of 50, 100, 200, 500 and 1000 were
introduced in 2012 (old and new coins
were valid at the time of writing); there
are notes of 1000, 2000, 5000, 10,000,
20,000 and 50,000 pesos (the latter can
be difficult to change). Change is in short
supply, especially in small towns, and in the
morning. Watch out for forged notes. The
50,000-peso note should smudge colour if
it is real; if not, refuse to accept it. There is a
limit of US$10,000 on the import of foreign
exchange in cash, with export limited to the
equivalent of the amount brought in.

Exchange

Cash and TCs can in theory be exchanged in any bank, except the **Banco de la República**; go early to banks in smaller places to change these. In most sizeable towns there are *casas de cambio* (exchange shops), which are quicker to use than banks but sometimes charge higher commission. It's best to use euros and, even better, dollars. It can be difficult to buy and sell large amounts of sterling. Hotels may give very poor rates of exchange. Hotels are not allowed to accept dollars as payment by law. Some may open a credit card account and give you cash on that. It is dangerous to change money on the streets and you may well be given counterfeit pesos, or robbed. Also in circulation are counterfeit US dollar bills. You must present your original passport when changing money (it will be photocopied and you may be fingerprinted, too). Take some US$ cash with you for emergencies.

Credit cards

It is unwise to carry large quantities of cash as credit cards are widely used, especially MasterCard and Visa; Diners Club is also accepted. American Express is only accepted in expensive places in Bogotá. Many banks accept Visa (Visaplus and ATH logos) and Cirrus/MasterCard (Maestro and Multicolor logos) to advance pesos against the card, or through ATMs. There are ATMs for Visa and MasterCard everywhere but you may have to try several machines. All **Exito** supermarkets have ATMs. ATMs do not retain cards – follow the instructions on screen. If your card is not given back immediately, do not proceed with the transaction and do not type in your pin number. There are reports of money being stolen from accounts when cards have been retained. ATMs dispense a frustratingly small amount of cash at a time. The maximum withdrawal is often 300,000 pesos (about US$165), which can accrue heavy bank charges over a period of time. For larger amounts try: **Davivienda** (500,000 per visit) and **Bancolombia** (400,000 per visit).

Note Only use ATMs in supermarkets, malls or where a security guard is present. Don't ask a taxi driver to wait while you use an ATM. Be particularly vigilant around Christmas time when thieves may be on the prowl.

Currency cards

If you don't want to carry lots of cash, prepaid currency cards allow you to preload money from your bank account, fixed at the day's exchange rate. They look like a credit or debit card and are issued by specialist money-changing companies, such as Travelex and Caxton FX. You can top up and check your balance by phone, online and sometimes by text.

Traveller's cheques

When changing TCs, you will need to show your passport and you may be asked for a photocopy (take a supply of photocopies with you). The procedure is always slow, sometimes involving finger printing and photographs. The best currency to take is US$; preferably in small denominations. Banks may be unwilling to change TCs in remote areas, so always have some local currency (and US$ for emergencies). TCs are not normally accepted in hotels, restaurants or shops.

Cost of living

Prices are a little lower than Europe and North America for services and locally produced items, but more expensive for imported and luxury goods. Modest, basic accommodation will cost about US$12-20 per person per night in Cartagena, Santa Marta and colonial cities, but a few dollars less elsewhere. A *menú ejecutivo* (set lunch) costs about US$3.50-5.50 and breakfast US$2-3. *A la carte* meals are usually good value and fierce competition for transport keeps prices low. Typical cost of internet is US$1-4 per hr.

Opening hours

Business hours depend a lot on where you are, so enquire locally. Generally offices are open Mon-Fri 0800-1700, but in hotter zones may close for lunch, 1200-1400, closing 1830 or 1900. Shops open 0700 or 0800 till 2000 and on Sat, but may close for lunch; supermarkets have longer hours and are open on Sat and Sun, usually 0900-1900. Banking hours: Mon-Thu 0900-1500, 1530 on Fri. Most businesses such as banks and airline offices close for official holidays while supermarkets and street markets may stay open.

Police and the law

You must carry identification at all times (see Visas, below). In the event of a vehicle accident in which anyone is injured, all drivers involved are usually detained until blame has been established, which may take several weeks. Never offer to bribe a police officer. If an official suggests that a bribe must be paid before you can proceed on your way, be patient and they may relent. In general, however, there are few hassles and most police are helpful to travellers.

Public holidays

1 Jan New Year's Day
6 Jan Epiphany*
19 Mar St Joseph*
Easter Maundy Thursday; Good Friday
1 May Labour Day
May Ascension Day* (6 weeks and a day after Easter Sunday)
May/Jun Corpus Christi* (9 weeks and a day after Easter Sunday)
Jun Sacred Heart* (movable)
29 Jun Saint Peter and Saint Paul*
20 Jul Independence Day
7 Aug Battle of Boyacá
15 Aug Assumption*
12 Oct Columbus' arrival in America* (Día de la Raza)
1 Nov All Saints' day*
11 Nov Independence of Cartagena*
8 Dec Immaculate Conception
25 Dec Christmas Day

When those marked with an asterisk (*) do not fall on a Mon, they will be moved to the following Mon. Public holidays are known as *puentes* (bridges).

Safety

The vast majority of Colombians are polite, honest and will go out of their way to help visitors and make them feel welcome. In general, anti-gringo sentiments are rare.

Drugs and scams

Colombia is part of a major drug-smuggling route. Police and customs activities have greatly intensified and smugglers increasingly try to use innocent carriers. Do not carry packages for other people. Hotels are sometimes checked by the police for drugs. Make sure they do not remove any of your belongings. You do not need to show them any money. Cooperate but be firm about your rights.

There have been reports of travellers being victims of *burundanga*, a drug obtained from a white flower, native to Colombia. At present, the use of this drug appears to be confined to major cities. It is very nasty, almost impossible to see or smell. It leaves the victim helpless and at the will of the culprit. Usually, the victim is taken to ATMs to draw out money. Be wary of accepting cigarettes, food and drink from strangers at sports events or on buses. In bars watch your drinks very carefully.

Other Colombian scams may involve fake police and taxicabs and there are variations in most major cities.

Guerrillas

The internal armed conflict in Colombia is almost impossible to predict and the security situation changes from day to day. For this reason, it is essential to consult regularly with locals for up-to-date information. Taxi and bus drivers, local journalists, soldiers at checkpoints, hotel owners and Colombians who actually travel around their country are usually good sources of reliable information.

Travelling overland between towns has in general become much safer due to increased military and police presence along main roads. Do not travel at night, though. In some areas, however, fighting between the armed forces and guerrilla groups continues even though, at the time of writing, peace talks between FARC and government are taking place. For the purposes of this guide, only the area from **Urabá** near the border with **Panamá** into northwestern **Antioquia** and the border with Venezuela are considered *zonas calientes* (hot zones) where there may be significant unrest. Many other parts of the country are also regarded as *zonas calientes*, so if travelling beyond Cartagena and the Caribbean, make full enquiries when moving on. Hotels and hostels favoured by travellers are good places to ask.

Hotel security

The cheapest hotels are usually found near markets and bus stations but these are also the least safe areas. Look for something a little better if you can afford it; if you must stay in a suspect area, try to return to your hotel before dark. If you trust your hotel, then you can leave any valuables you don't need in their safe-deposit box, but always keep an inventory of what you have deposited. An alternative to leaving valuables with the hotel administration is to lock everything in your pack and secure that in your room. Even in an apparently safe hotel, never leave valuable objects strewn about your room.

Theft

Pickpockets, bag snatchers and bag slashers are always a hazard for tourists, especially in crowded areas such as markets or the downtown cores of major cities. You should likewise avoid deserted areas, such as parks or plazas after hours. Be especially careful arriving at or leaving from bus stations. As a rule these are often the most dangerous areas of most towns and are obvious places to catch people carrying a lot of important belongings.

Leave unnecessary documents and valuables at home. Those you bring should be carried in a money-belt or pouch, including your passport, airline tickets, credit and debit cards. Hide your main cash supply in several different places. Never carry valuables in an ordinary pocket, purse or day-pack. Keep cameras in bags or day-packs and generally out of sight. Do not wear expensive wrist watches or jewellery. If you are wearing a shoulder-bag or day-pack in a crowd, carry it in front of you.

Women travellers

Unaccompanied foreign women may be objects of some curiosity. Don't be unduly scared – or flattered. Avoid arriving anywhere after dark. Remember that for a single woman a taxi at night can be as dangerous as wandering around alone. If you accept a social invitation, make sure that someone knows the address and the time you left. Ask if you can bring a friend (even if you do not). As elsewhere, watch your alcohol intake at parties with locals, especially if you are on your own. A good general rule is to always look confident and pretend you know where you are going, even if you do not. Don't tell strangers where you are staying.

Taxes
Airport taxes

The airport departure tax in most Colombian airports is about US$35, payable in dollars or pesos; see www.elnuevodorado.com/tramites.html. In Caribbean airports, however, the tax is much higher: US$92 at Cartagena (see www.sacsa.co), US$87 at Santa Marta and US$86 at Barranquilla (see www.aerocivil.gov.co). It is usually included in the ticket price, but check. Travellers changing planes in Colombia and leaving the same day are exempt from this tax. When you arrive, ensure that all necessary documentation bears a stamp for your date of arrival. There is also an airport tax on internal flights, about US$6 at Cartagena

(US$5 at other airports), usually included in the ticket price.

VAT

16%. Ask for an official receipt if you want it documented. Some hotels and restaurants add *IVA* (VAT) onto bills. Strictly speaking foreigners should be exempt from this, but there seems to be some confusion about the application of this law. Raise the matter with your hotel and you may well get a discount. Some hotels add a small insurance charge.

Telephone → *Country code T+57.*
Ringing: equal tones with long pauses. Engaged: short tones with short pauses. National and international calls can be made from public phone offices in all major cities and rural towns. You are assigned a cabin in which to make your calls; pay on the way out. You can also make calls from street vendors who hire out mobile phones (usually signposted '*minutos*'). For call boxes, phone cards are the best option. It is relatively inexpensive to buy a pay-as-you-go SIM card for your mobile phone. Mobile phone numbers start with a 3-digit prefix beginning with 3.

Time

GMT -5 all year round.

Tourist information

National tourism is part of the Ministry of Commerce, Industry and Tourism, C 28, No 13A-15, Bogotá, www.mincomercio. gov.co, with its portal, **Proexport**, at the same address, p 35-36, T560 0100, www.colombia.travel. Departmental and city entities have their own offices responsible for tourist information; see the text for local details. These offices should be visited as early as possible for information on accommodation and transport, but also for details on areas that are dangerous to visit. Otherwise contact Colombia's representation overseas.

The **National Parks Service** is at the Ministerio del Medio Ambiente, Vivienda y Desarrollo Territorial (Ministry of the Environment, www.minambiente.gov.co), Ecotourism office, Carrera 10, No 20-30, p 1, Bogotá, T01-353 2400, Mon-Fri 0745-1745, www.parquesnacionales.gov.co (which has a list of regional offices). Staff can provide information about facilities and accommodation, and have maps. Some parks and protected areas require permits to visit; check with the head office where these must be obtained before going to the park. Do not go directly to the parks themselves. Some prices vary according to high and low seasons. High season includes: weekends, Jun-Jul, Dec-Jan, public holidays and Semana Santa. **Aviatur** travel agency, Av 19, No 4-62, Bogotá, T381 7111, www.concesionesparquesnaturales.com, has the concession for accommodation in Tayrona (address given in text, not always efficient). Foreigners over 18 can participate on the voluntary park ranger programme. Details are available from the Ecotourism office in Bogotá. You will have to provide photocopies of ID documents and Colombian entry stamp in your passport. A good level of Spanish is required.

The **Asociación Red Colombiana de Reservas Naturales de la Sociedad Civil**, Cra 71C, No 122-72, Bogotá, T313-357 4406, www.resnatur.org.co, is a network of privately owned nature reserves that works with local people to build a sustainable model of environmentally friendly tourism.

Conservation websites

www.colparques.net Organización para la Promoción de los Parques Naturales de Colombia.
www.humboldt.org.co Site of Institute Von Humboldt, probably the most important environment research organization in Colombia. An excellent site with descriptions of the different ecosystems in the country and projects with ethnic communities (in Spanish).

www.natura.org.co Fundación Natura, excellent conservation information.
www.proaves.org Fundación ProAves, an NGO dedicated to the study and conservation of birds and their habitats; publishes a good *Field Guide to the Birds of Colombia*.

Useful websites
www.experienciacolombia.com Tourism website.
www.ideam.gov.co Weather forecasts and climate information, in Spanish and English.
www.presidencia.gov.co The government website. You can also access: **www.gobierno enlinea.gov.co**, in Spanish and English.

Visas and immigration
Tourists are allowed to stay a maximum of 180 days in a calendar year. Make sure that, on entry, you are granted enough days for your visit. On entry you are given 90 days. If you wish to extend your permission to stay in Colombia, for a further 90 days, apply 2-3 days before your permit expires at a Centro Facilitador de Servicios Migratorios (CFSM) of **Migración Colombia** (www.migracioncolombia.gov.co gives a full list); it costs about US$32. Take 2 copies of your passport details, the original entry stamp, 2 passport photos and a copy of your ticket out of Colombia. This does not apply to visas. If you overstay an entry permit or visa, a *salvoconducto* can be applied for at a CFSM. The *salvoconducto* is only issued once for a period of 30 days and is usually processed within 24 hrs; it costs about US$19. Take 2 recent photos and copies of your passport. The Migración Colombia head office in Bogotá is at C 100, No 11B-27, T511 1150, www.migracioncolombia.gov.co (see also under Directory sections for other cities). Arrive early in the morning, expect long queues and a painfully slow bureaucratic process. **Note** Migración Colombia does not accept cash payments; these are made at the branches of Banco de Occidente with special payments slips (in Maicao, use Banco de Bogotá). An onward ticket may be asked for at land borders or Bogotá international airport. You may be asked to prove that you have sufficient funds for your stay.

To visit Colombia as a tourist, nationals of most Western countries do not need a visa. Nationals of the Middle East (except Israel), Asian countries (except Japan, South Korea, Phillipines, Indonesia and Singapore), Bulgaria, Haiti, Nicaragua, and all African countries (except South Africa) need a visa. Always check for changes in regulations before leaving your home country.
Tourist visas are issued only by Colombian consulates. When a visa is required you must present a valid passport, 3 photographs on white background, the application form (in duplicate), US$17-40 or equivalent (price varies according to nationality), onward tickets, and a photocopy of all the documents (allow 2 weeks maximum). A non-refundable charge of US$50 is made for any study made by the Colombian authorities prior to a visa being issued.

If you are going to take a Spanish course, you must have a **student visa** (US$40, plus US$15 charge), valid for 1 year. You may not study on a tourist visa. A student visa can be obtained while in Colombia on a tourist visa. Proof of sufficient funds is necessary. You must be first enrolled in a course from a bona fide university to apply for a student visa.

Various **business visas** and other temporary visas are needed for foreigners who have to reside in Colombia for a length of time. The **Ministerio de Relaciones Exteriores**, C 10, No 5-51, Bogotá, T381 4000, www.cancilleria. gov.co, Mon-Fri 0800-1700, processes student and some work visas. In general, Colombian work visas can only be obtained outside Colombia at the appropriate consulate or embassy. You must register work and student visas at a Migración Colombia office within 15 days of obtaining them, otherwise you will be liable to pay a hefty fine. Visas must be used within 3 months. Supporting documentary requirements for visas change frequently.

Check with the appropriate consulate in good time before your trip.

When entering the country, you will be given the copy of your *DIAN* (Customs) luggage declaration. Keep it; you may be asked for it when you leave. If you receive an entry card when flying in and lose it while in Colombia, apply to any Migración Colombia office who should issue one and restamp your passport for free. Normally passports are scanned by a computer and no landing card is issued, but passports still must be stamped on entry. Note that to leave Colombia you must get an exit stamp from the Migración Colombia. They often do not have offices at the small border towns, so try to get your stamp in a main city.

Note It is highly recommended that you photocopy your passport details, including entry stamps which, for added insurance, you can have witnessed by a notary. Always carry a photocopy of your passport with you, as you may be asked for identification. This is a valid substitute for most purposes though not, for example, for cashing TCs or drawing cash across a bank counter. Generally acceptable for identification (eg to enter government buildings) is a driving licence, provided it is plastic, of credit card size and has a photograph. For more information, check with your consulate.

Weights and measures
Colombia uses the metric system, but US gallons for petrol.

Contents

Footprint features

Cartagena & Caribbean Coast

Cartagena

Cartagena is one of the hottest, most vibrant and beautiful cities in South America, combining as it does superb weather, a sparkling stretch of the Caribbean and an abundance of tropical fruits. Nuggets of history can be found around every corner and in every palm-shaded courtyard of this most romantic of places. With exquisitely preserved colonial mansions, excellent museums and fine dining, it's a place not to be missed.

Besides being Colombia's top tourist destination and a World Heritage Site, it has an eclectic mix of Caribbean, African and Spanish tastes and sounds. The colonial heart of Cartagena lies within 12 km of ramparts. The walled city, El Centro, is a labyrinth of colourful squares, churches, mansions of former nobles and pastel-coloured houses along narrow cobbled streets. Most of the upmarket hotels and restaurants are found here. The San Diego quarter, once home to the middle classes, and Plaza Santo Domingo perhaps best capture the lure of Cartagena. Less touristy and developed is the poorer Getsemaní neighbourhood, where colonial buildings of former artisans are being rapidly restored and most of the budget hotels are to be found. Immediately adjoining Getsemaní is the downtown sector known as La Matuna.

Cartagena is also a popular beach resort and along Bocagrande and El Laguito are modern high-rise hotels on the seafront. Beyond Crespo on the road to Barranquilla is a fast-growing beach resort lined with luxury apartments.

During the high season the walled city becomes a playground for the rich and famous, while cruise liners dock at its port. Don't miss a drink at night in the cafés next to the city's oldest church, Santo Domingo, and in Plaza San Diego.

Arriving in Cartagena → *Phone code: 5.*

Getting there

Rafael Núñez Airport is 1.5 km from the city in the Crespo district and it can be reached by local buses from Blas de Lezo, in the southwest corner of the inner wall. A bus from the airport to Plaza San Francisco costs US$1. A taxi to San Diego or the centre is US$5 and to Bocagrande US$8.50. City buses can be very crowded so if you have a lot of luggage, a taxi is recommended. There is a *casa de cambio* (T656 4943, Monday-Friday 0830-2030, Saturday 0830-1700, Sunday 0830-2100) at the airport but rates are better in town. Travel agents have offices on the upper level. There is also a good self-service restaurant.

The **bus terminal** ① *www.terminaldecartagena.com*, is at least 35 minutes away from town on the road to Barranquilla, a taxi costs US$9, or you can take the Metrocar city buses to the 'Terminal de Transportes', US$1. Agree your taxi fare before you get in.

Undoubtedly the best way to arrive is by sea and a description of the approach is given below, under Background. Regular lines are at present non-existent, but Cartagena is popular for cruise ships and those who have their own sea transport: around 345,000 passengers pass through the docks each year. Equally, many tourists take trips to the offshore islands. ⇥ *See Transport, page 42.*

Getting around

Local buses Within the city large buses (with no glass in the windows) cost US$0.75; air-conditioned buses charge US$1. Green and white **Metrocar** buses are a recommended way to get to all areas. **Taxis** are also quite cheap and more convenient than buses. There are no meters, journeys are calculated by zones, each zone costing about US$1.50, though the minimum fare is US$4 (eg Bocagrande to Centro, two zones, is still US$4). It is quite common to ask other people waiting if they would like to share, but, in any case, always agree the fare with the driver before getting in. By arrangement, taxis will wait for you if visiting more remote places. Fares go up at night.

Best time to visit

The climate varies little during the year. Temperatures rise marginally when there is more frequent rain (August-November), and there can be flooding. Trade winds during December-February provide relief from the heat. Fiestas are taken seriously in Cartagena, and if you want a quiet time you might want to avoid certain times of the year. If you want to join in, be sure to plan in advance or be prepared to struggle for accommodation and expect higher prices. ⇥ *See Festivals, page 41.*

Tourist information

Turismo Cartagena de Indias ① *the main office is in the Casa del Marqués del Premio Real, Plaza de la Aduana, T660 1583, Mon, Wed, Thu, Sat 0800-1900, Tue 0800-1200, 1400-1800, Sun 0900-1700 (very helpful and knowledgeable staff), and there are kiosks in Plaza de los Coches and Plaza de San Pedro Claver, Mon-Sat 0900-1300, 1500-1900, the latter is also open Sun 0900-1700.* **Corporación de Turismo Cartagena de Indias** ① *Av Blas de Lezo, Muelle Turístico, La Bodeguita, p 2, T655 0277, www.cartagenadeindias.travel (by appointment only).* The **Instituto de Patrimonio y Cultura de Cartagena** ① *C del Tablón No 7-28, Edif Gonzales Porto, T664 5361, www.ipcc.gov.co,* may provide information. See also www.cartagenacaribe.com. For maps, contact **Instituto Agustín Codazzi** ① *C 34, No 3A-31, T664 4171, Edif Inurbe, www.igac.gov.co, Mon-Fri 0800-1630.* **This Is Cartagena,**

www.ticartagena.com, is an independent collective offering lots of practical information, entertainment listings, details of volunteering projects and more.

Security
Carry your passport, or a photocopy, at all times. Failure to present it on police request can result in imprisonment and fines. Generally, the central areas are safe and friendly (although Getsemaní is less secure), but should you require the police, there is a station in Barrio Manga. Beware of drug pushers on the beaches, pickpockets in crowded areas and bag/camera snatchers on quiet Sunday mornings. At the bus station, do not be pressurized into a hotel recommendation different from your own choice.

Background

The full name of Cartagena is Cartagena de Indias, a name that is quite frequently used and a reminder that the early Spanish navigators believed they had reached the Far East. It was founded by Pedro de Heredia on 13 January 1533. The core of the city was built by the Spaniards on an island separated from the mainland by marshes and lagoons close to a prominent hill, a perfect place for a harbour and, more important at the time, easy to defend against attack. Furthermore, it was close to the mouth of the Río Magdalena, the route to the interior of the continent. In 1650, the Spaniards built a connection to the river, 145 km long, known as the **Canal del Dique**, to allow free access for ships from the upriver ports. This waterway has been used on and off ever since, was updated in the early 19th century and it is still used, mainly by barges, today.

The great Bay of Cartagena, 15 km long and 5 km wide is protected by several low, sandy islands. There were then two approaches to it, Bocagrande, at the northern end of Tierrabomba island – this was the direct entry from the Caribbean – and Bocachica, a narrow channel to the south of the island. Bocagrande was blocked by an underwater wall after Admiral Vernon's attack in 1741, thus leaving only one, easily protected, entrance to the approach to the harbour. The old walled city lies at the north end of the Bahía de Cartagena.

Cartagena declared its Independence from Spain in 1811. A year later Bolívar used the city as a jumping-off point for his Magdalena campaign. After heroic resistance, Cartagena was retaken by the royalists under General Pablo Morillo in 1815. It was finally freed by the patriots in 1821.

Cartagena today
Although Cartagena is Colombia's fifth largest city, the short-term visitor will not be aware of the size of the place. Beyond and behind the old walled city, Bocagrande and Manga, is a large sprawling conurbation that stretches 10 km to the southeast. People have been moving in to add to the pressure on the poorer neighbourhoods as everywhere else in this part of the world, but Cartagena is a long way from the more heavily populated parts of highland Colombia, to the city's advantage.

Places in Cartagena → *For listings, see pages 36-43.*

The city's fortifications

Cartagena was one of the storage points for merchandise from Spain and for treasure collected from the Americas to be sent back. A series of forts protecting the approaches from the sea, and the formidable walls built around the city, made it almost impregnable.

Entering the **Bahía de Cartagena** by sea through Bocachica, the island of Tierrabomba is to the left. At the southern tip of Tierrabomba is the fortress of **San Fernando**. Opposite it, right on the end of Barú island, is the **Fuerte San José**. The two forts were once linked by heavy chains to prevent surprise attacks by pirates. Barú island is separated from the mainland only by the Canal del Dique. In recent years, the city has been expanding down the coast opposite Tierrabomba and settlements can be seen as you approach the entrance to the inner harbour of Cartagena, protected by another two forts, **San José de Manzanillo**, on the mainland, and the **Fuerte Castillo Grande** on the tip of **Bocagrande**, now the main beach resort of the city.

In the centre of the harbour is the statue of the Virgin with the port installations to the right on Manga Island. There is a very good view of the harbour, cruise boats and port activity from the end of Calle 6/Carrera 14, Bocagrande, though access to Castillo Grande itself is restricted. Manga Island is now an important suburb of the city. At its northern end a bridge, **Puente Román**, connects it with the old city. This approach to the city was defended by three forts: **San Sebastián del Pastelillo**, built between 1558 and 1567 (the Club de Pesca has it now), at the northwestern tip of Manga Island; the fortress of **San Lorenzo** near the city itself; and the very powerful **Castillo San Felipe de Barajas** ① *inland on San Lázaro hill, daily 0800-1800, US$4.50, guides available*, 41 m above sea level, to the east of the city.

The first of Cartagena's fortifications were built in 1536 though the main constructions began in 1639 and it was finished by 1657. It is the largest Spanish fort built in the Americas. Under the huge structure is a network of tunnels cut into the rock, lined with living rooms and offices. Some are open and illuminated, a flashlight will be handy in the others; visitors pass through these and on to the top of the fortress. Good footwear is advisable in the damp sloping tunnels. Baron de Pointis, the French pirate, stormed and took it, but Admiral Vernon failed to reach it. In the **Almacén de Pólvora** (Gunpowder store), there is an interesting 1996 reproduction of Vernon's map of the abortive attempt to take the city in 1741. On the statue of Don Blas de Lezo below the fortress, don't miss the plaque displaying the medal prematurely struck celebrating Vernon's 'victory'.

Yet another fort, **La Tenaza**, protected the northern point of the walled city from a direct attack from the open sea. The huge encircling walls were started early in the 17th century and finished by 1735. They were on average 12 m high and 17 m thick, with six gates. Besides barracks, they contained a water reservoir.

Around the old city

The old walled city was in two sections, outer and inner. Much of the wall between the two disappeared some years ago. Nearly all the houses are of one or two storeys. In the outer city, the artisan classes lived in the one-storey houses of **Getsemaní** where many colonial buildings survive. Today, there is a concentration of hotels and restaurants here. Immediately adjoining is the modern downtown sector, known as **La Matuna**, where vendors crowd the pavements and alleys between the modern commercial buildings. Several middle range hotels are in this district, between Avenidas Venezuela and Lemaitre.

Cartagena historical centre

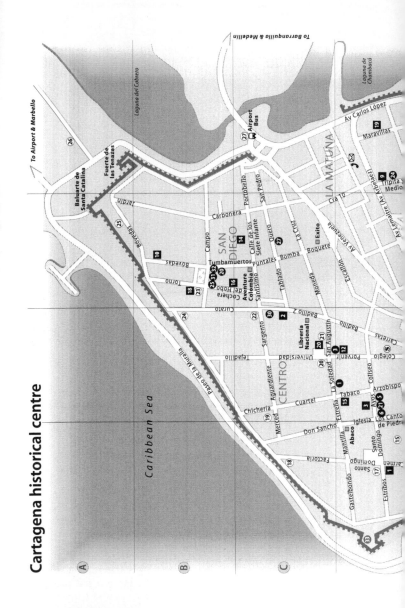

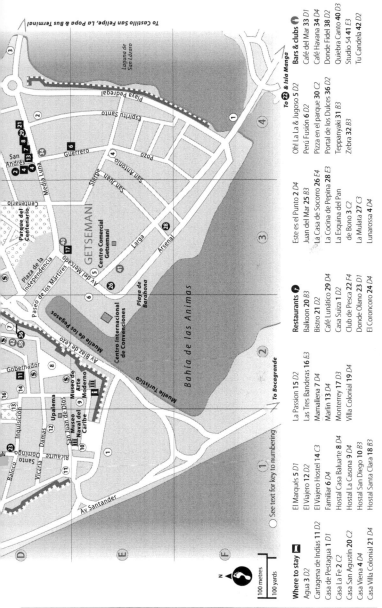

To Castillo San Felipe, La Popa & Bus Terminal

Laguna de
San Lázaro

San
Andrés

Playa Pedregal

Espíritu Santo

Guerrero

GETSEMANÍ

Pozo

San Antonio

Sierpe

San Juan

Media Luna

Centenario

Parque del
Centenario

Plaza de la
Independencia

Paseo de los Mártires

Av del Mercado

Larga

Arsenal

Centro Comercial
Getsemaní

Playa de
Barahona

Muelle de los Pegasos

Paseo de los Mártires

Centro Internacional
de Convenciones

Av Blas de Lezo

Bahía de las Ánimas

Muelle Turístico

To Bocagrande

Gobernador

Museo de
Arte
Moderno

San Juan de Dios

Museo
Naval del
Caribe

Upalema

Inquisición

Damas

Santo Domingo

Ricaurte

Vicaria

Balco

Av Santander

To ② & Isla Manga

N

100 metres
100 yards

○ See text for key to numbering

Where to stay 🛏
Agua 3 D2
Cartagena de Indias 11 D2
Casa de Pestagua 1 D1
Casa La Fe 2 C2
Casa San Agustín 20 C2
Casa Viena 4 D4
Casa Villa Colonial 21 D4
El Marqués 5 D1
El Viajero 12 D2
El Viajero Hostel 14 C3
Familiar 6 D4
Hostal Casa Baluarte 8 D4
Hostal La Casona 9 D4
Hostal San Diego 10 B3
Hostal Santa Clara 18 B3
La Passion 15 D1
Las Tres Banderas 16 E3
Mamallena 7 D4
Marlin 13 D4
Monterrey 17 D3
Villa Colonial 19 D4

Restaurants 🍴
Balkoon 20 B3
Bistro 21 D2
Café Lunático 29 D4
Casa Suiza 1 D2
Club de Pesca 22 F4
Donde Olano 23 D1
El Coroncoro 24 D4
Este es el Punto 2 D4
Juan del Mar 25 B3
La Casa de Socorro 26 E4
La Cocina de Pepina 28 E3
La Esquina del Pan
de Bono 3 C2
La Mulata 27 C3
Lunarossa 4 D4
Ohl La La & Jugoso 5 D2
Perú Fusión 6 D2
Pizza en el parque 30 D2
Portal de los Dulces 36 D2
Teppanyaki 31 B3
Zebra 32 B3

Bars & clubs 🍸
Café del Mar 33 D1
Café Havana 34 D4
Donde Fidel 38 D2
Quiebra Canto 40 D3
Studio 54 41 E3
Tu Candela 42 D2

In the **inner** city, the houses in **El Centro** were originally occupied by the high officials and nobility. **San Diego** (the northern end of the inner city) was where the middle classes lived: the clerks, merchants, priests and military.

Just under a kilometre from the old city, along a seafront boulevard, **Bocagrande** is a spit of land crowded with hotel and apartment towers. Thousands of visitors flock to the beach with its accompanying resort atmosphere, fast-food outlets, shops – and dirty seawater. ▸▸ *See Beaches, page 35.*

The old city streets are narrow. Each block has a different name, a source of confusion, but don't worry: the thing to do is to wander aimlessly, savouring the street scenes, and allow the great sights to catch you by surprise. However, if you do want to know what you are looking at, the maps are marked with numerals for the places of outstanding interest. Most of the 'great houses' can be visited. Churches are generally open to the public at 1800, some for most of the day. Weekends and holidays are the best time for photography when traffic is minimal. What follows is a walking route for the sights of the old city which you can pick up and leave wherever you wish. Note that the numbers below refer to the circled numbers on the Historical Centre map.

Outer city

The **Puente Román** (**1**) is the bridge which leads from Manga Island, with its shipping terminals, into Getsemaní, characterized by its *casas bajas* (low houses). The chapel of **San Roque** (**2**), early 17th century, is near the end of Calle Media Luna, and the hospital of Espíritu Santo. Just across the Playa Pedregal (**3**) is the Laguna de San Lázaro and the **Puente Heredia**, on the other side of which is the Castillo San Felipe de Barajas, see above. In an interesting plaza, is the church of **La Trinidad** (**4**), built 1643 but not consecrated until 1839. Near the church, at No 10 Calle Guerrero, lived Pedro Romero, who set the revolution of 1811 going by coming out into the street shouting 'Long Live Liberty'. His statue can be seen outside La Trinidad. Along Calle Larga (**5**), Calle 25, is the monastery of **San Francisco**. The church was built in 1590 after the pirate Martin Côte had destroyed an earlier church built in 1559. The first Inquisitors lodged at the monastery. From its courtyard a crowd surged into the streets claiming Independence from Spain on 11 November 1811. The main part of the monastery has now been turned into business premises – take a look at the cloister garden as you pass by. Good-value fixed-price handicrafts are sold in the grounds of the monastery and, at the back, is the Centro Comercial Getsemaní, a busy shopping centre. On the corner of Calle Larga, formerly part of the Franciscan complex, is the **Iglesia de la Tercera Orden**, a busy church with a fine wooden roof of unusual design and some brightly painted niche figures. The church and monastery front on to the Avenida del Mercado on the other side of which is the **Centro Internacional de Convenciones** (**6**). It holds gatherings of up to 4000 people and is frequently used for local and international conventions. It was built in 1972 on the site of the old colourful market, now banished to the interior part of the city. Although the severe fort-like structure is more or less in keeping with the surrounding historic walls and bastions, not everyone believes this is an improvement. When not in use, ask for a guide to show you around.

Immediately to the north is **Plaza de la Independencia**, with the landscaped **Parque del Centenario** alongside. Alongside the plaza, by the water, runs the **Paseo de los Mártires**, flanked by the busts of nine patriots executed in the square on 24 February 1816 by the royalist Pablo Morillo after he had retaken the city.

Inner city

At the western end of the Paseo is a tall clock tower, Torre del Reloj, often used as the symbol of Cartagena. To the left is the **Muelle de los Pegasos** (Muelle Turístico) from where the tourist boats leave. Under the clock tower is the **Puerta del Reloj** and the three arches are the principal entrance to the inner walled city. Inside is the **Plaza de los Coches** (**7**). As with almost all the plazas of Cartagena, arcades here offer refuge from the tropical sun. At one time, this plaza was the slave market, and later, it was from here that carriages (*coches*) could be hired for local journeys. On the west side of this plaza is the **Portal de los Dulces**, a favourite meeting place and where you can still buy all manner of local sweets and delicacies. It also has a number of good bars, often quite buzzing even during the day. **Plaza de la Aduana** (**8**), with a statue of Columbus in the centre and the **Casa de la Aduana** along the wall, originally the tax office and now part of the city administration as the **Palacio Municipal**. Opposite is the **Casa del Marqués del Premio Real** which was the residence of the representative of the Spanish king. In the corner of the wall is the **Museo de Arte Moderno** ① *Mon-Sat 0900-1200, 1500-1800, US$3.50*, a collection of the work of modern Colombian artists. There is a museum shop.

Past the museum is the **Convento de San Pedro Claver** (**9**) ① *Mon-Fri 0800-1730, Sat 0800-1600 US$4.25*, and the church and monastery of the same name, built by Jesuits in 1603 and later dedicated to San Pedro Claver, a monk in the monastery, who died in 1654 and was canonized 235 years later. He was called *El Esclavo de los Esclavos*, or *El Apóstol de los Negros*: he used to beg from door to door for money to give to the black slaves brought to the city. His body is in an illuminated glass coffin set in the high marble altar, and his cell and the balcony from which he kept watch for slave ships are shown to visitors. There are brightly coloured birds in the small monastery garden. Several upstairs rooms form a museum, with many interesting items linked or unrelated to Pedro Claver. In the pottery room, for example, is the chair used by the Pope on his visit to Cartagena in 1986. In another room there are several old maps, one of which shows the Caribbean maritime boundaries of Colombia, topical in that disputes with Nicaragua over San Andrés still persist in 2013, despite an international court ruling in favour of Colombia.

Following the wall round, it is well worthwhile climbing up the **Baluarte San Francisco Javier** (**10**) for a good view of the city and the Caribbean. There is a **Museo Naval del Caribe** ① *C San Juan de Dios No3-62, T5-664 2440, www.museonavaldelcaribe.com, daily 1000-1730, US$3*, with maps, models and displays of armaments, near the Baluarte. On the corner of Calle Ricaurte is the convent of **Santa Teresa** (**11**), founded in 1609 by a rich benefactor as a convent for Carmelite nuns. It had various uses subsequently, as a prison, a military barracks, a school and in the 1970s, was occupied by the police. It was purchased by the Banco Central as a heritage investment and has been converted into a hotel, the **Charleston Santa Teresa** ① *Cra 3, No 31-23, www.hotelcharlestonsantateresa.com*. It is possible to visit the public areas of the hotel and admire the tasteful work of restoration. There is a great view from the roof.

El Bodegón de la Candelaria (**12**) ① *C Las Damas No 3-64*, was an elegant colonial residence. It has been faithfully restored and there is some fine panelling and period furniture to see. A small shrine in one of the rooms marks the place where the Virgin appeared to a priest who was living there at the time. One block away is **Plaza de Bolívar** (**13**) with an equestrian statue of the Liberator in the centre. Formerly it was the Plaza de la Inquisición, with the Palacio de la Inquisición (see below), on its west side. The gardens of the plaza are an attractive corner of Cartagena.

On the opposite side of the Plaza de Bolívar to the Palacio de la Inquisición is the **Museo del Oro Zenú (14)** ① *www.banrepcultural.org/gold-museum/regional-museums, Tue-Sat 1000-1300, 1500-1800, free.* Gold and pottery are very well displayed. Specially featured is the Zenú area to the south of Cartagena in the marshlands of the Sinú, San Jorge and Magdalena rivers, which is flooded by the river waters six to eight months of the year. Early drainage systems are featured, as is the advanced level of weaving techniques using the *cañafleche* and other fresh water reeds. This area was densely populated between the second and 10th centuries during which time the gold working skills of the people were developed to the high level that can still be seen today at Mompós, at the northern edge of the Zenú region.

The **Palacio de La Inquisición (15)** ① *Mon-Sat 0900-1900, Sun 0900-1600, US$6.75*, is on the other side of the Plaza Bolívar. The jurisdiction of this tribunal extended to Venezuela and Panama, and at least 800 were sentenced to death here. There is a small window overlooking the plaza where the public were informed of the sentences. First established in 1610, the present building dates from 1706. The stone entrance with its coats of arms and ornate wooden door is well preserved. The whole building, with its balconies, cloisters and patios, is a fine example of colonial baroque. It has been restored with air-conditioned rooms. The small museum contains photos of Cartagena from the 20th century, paintings of historical figures and a torture chamber (with reproductions of actual instruments). Of special interest are the model of Cartagena in 1808, copies of Alexander Von Humboldt's maps showing the link he discovered between the Orinoco and Amazon rivers (*Canal de Casiquiare*) and of the Maypures rapids on the Orinoco – note that the longitude lines on the maps are west of Paris not Greenwich.

The **cathedral (16)**, in the northeast corner of Plaza de Bolívar, begun in 1575, was partially destroyed by Francis Drake. Reconstruction was finished by 1612. Great alterations were made between 1912 and 1923. It has a severe exterior, with a fine doorway, and a simply decorated interior. See the gilded 18th-century altar, the Carrara marble pulpit and the elegant arcades which sustain the central nave.

Across the street is the **Palacio de la Proclamación** named for the declaration of Independence of the State of Cartagena in November 1811. Before that it was the local governor's residence, and later where Simón Bolívar stayed in 1826. The building was restored in 1950. The adjacent plaza has interesting local art and sculpture on display daily in high season.

The church and monastery of **Santo Domingo (17)**, built 1570 to 1579 is now a seminary. The old monastery was replaced by the present one in the 17th century. Inside, a miracle-making image of Christ, carved towards the end of the 16th century, is set on a baroque 19th-century altar. This is a most interesting neighbourhood, where very little has changed since the 16th century. In Calle Santo Domingo, No 33-29, is one of the great patrician houses of Cartagena, the **Casa de los Condes de Pestagua**, until recently the Colegio del Sagrado Corazón de Jesús, now a boutique hotel (see page 37). It has a fine colonnaded courtyard, marble floors and magnificent palm trees in the centre garden. Beside the church is the **Plaza de Santo Domingo**, one of the favourite corners of Cartagena, with popular restaurants, bars and cafés. A sculpture by Fernando Botero, *Gertrudis*, or *La Gorda*, is in the plaza, presenting an interesting juxtaposition between the colonial and the modern.

North of Santo Domingo at Calle de la Factoría 36-57 is the magnificent **Casa del Marqués de Valdehoyos (18)**, originally owned by the Marqués, who had the lucrative licences to import slaves and flour. The woodcarving is some of the best in Cartagena and the ceilings, chandeliers, wooden arches and balustrading are unique. The views of the city from the fine upper floor balconies are also recommended. It is used for cultural events and conferences.

A short walk north is the plaza, church and convent of **La Merced** (**19**), founded 1618. The convent was a prison during Morillo's reign of terror. Its church is now the **Teatro Heredia**, which has been beautifully restored.

Two blocks east is Calle de la Universidad, at the end of which is the monastery of **San Agustín** (**20**), built in 1580, currently the Universidad de Cartagena. From its chapel, the pirate Baron de Pointis stole a 500-pound silver sepulchre. It was returned by the King of France but the citizens melted it down to pay their troops during the siege by Morillo in 1815. There is a luxury hotel **Casa San Agustín** ① *C de la Universidad No 36-44, www.hotelcasasanagustin.com*.

One block along Calle de San Agustín is **La Casa Museo de Simón Bolívar** (**21**), a collection of memorabilia in the first Cartagena house he stayed in, now part of the **Biblioteca Bartolomé Calvo** owned by the Banco de la República.

One block along Badillo (Carrera 7) is the church of **Santo Toribio de Mogrovejo** (**22**) ① *opens for Mass Mon-Fri 0630, 1200, 1815, Sat 0630, 1200, 1800 and Sun 0800, 1000, 1800, 1900, closed at other times*. Building began in 1729. In 1741, during Admiral Vernon's siege, a cannon ball fell into the church during Mass and lodged in one of the central columns; the ball is now in a recess in the west wall. The font of Carrara marble in the Sacristy is a masterpiece. There is a beautiful carved ceiling (*mudéjar* style) above the main altar with a rear lighted figure of Christ.

The church and monastery of **Santa Clara de Assisi** (**23**) is close by. It was built 1617-1621, and has been spectacularly restored. It is now a hotel (**Santa Clara** ① *C del Torno, No 39-29, www.sofitel.com*), but this is one you must see. Behind the hotel is the orange **Casa de Gabriel García Márquez** (**24**), the most famous living Colombian author, on the corner of Calle del Curato.

Beyond the Santa Clara is the **Plaza de Las Bóvedas** (**25**). Towards the sea, before Las Bóvedas, you will see a bank (*espiga*) leading to a jetty used in colonial times when the water came up to the walls, as shown on the 1808 map displayed in the **Palacio de la Inquisición**. All the land below the walls has since been reclaimed, with sports fields, recreational areas and the Avenida Santander/Paseo de la Muralla, a busy bypass to the city. The walls of Las Bóvedas, built 1799, are 12 m high and 15-18 m thick. At the base of the wall are 23 dungeons, now containing tourist shops. Both an illuminated underground passage and a drawbridge lead from Las Bóvedas to the fortress of La Tenaza, which guarded the approach to the city from the coast to the northeast. In the neighbouring Baluarte de Santa Catalina is the **Museo Fortificación de Santa Catalina** ① *www.fortificacionesde cartagena.com, daily 0800-1800, US$3.60, children US$2*, inside the city walls.

Casa de Núñez (**26**) ① *Tue-Sat 0900-1730, Sun 1300-1600, US$2*, just outside the walls of La Tenaza in El Cabrero district, was the home of Rafael Núñez, four-time president of Colombia. He wrote the national anthem and established the constitution of 1886, to which there is a monument in the small park beside the lagoon. Núñez' grandiose marble tomb is in the delightful small **Ermita El Cabrero** church opposite.

Closer to the centre, where the main road leads into the city, is a roundabout, in the centre of which is the monument to **La India Catalina** (**27**), Pedro de Heredia's indigenous interpreter in the early days of the Spanish conquest. A miniature of this statue is given to the winner of the annual Cartagena film festival – a Colombian 'Oscar'.

The ramparts

In addition to being a spectacular feature of Cartagena, the city walls make a great walk and are an excellent way to visit many of the attractions inside (see www.fortificacionesdecartagena.com). A good place to start is the **Baluarte San Francisco Javier** (**10**) from where, with a few ups and downs, it is continuous to **La India Catalina** (**28**). From this point, there are two further sections along the lagoons to the **Puente Román** (**1**). The final section along the Calle del Arsenal can be completed through the **Playa de Barahona**, a bayside park, which is busy at weekends. The entire walk takes about 1½ hours, although if you take a camera it can take considerably longer. It is a spectacular walk in the morning around 0600 and equally at sunset. At many points you can drop down to see the sights detailed above in the tour of the old city.

Three of Cartagena's sights are off our map. Two of them, the Fortress of San Fernando and the Castillo San Felipe de Barajas, across the **Puente Heredia** (**3**) have been described above. The third is **Convento La Popa** ① *daily 0830-1730, US$4.60, children and students US$2, guides available*, on La Popa hill, nearly 150 m high, from where there is a fine view of the harbour and the city. It is not recommended to walk up on your own; either take a guided tour or take a public bus to Teatro Miramar at the foot of the hill (US$1), then bargain for a taxi up, about US$12 return (US$30 from centre of town with wait). The Augustinian church and monastery of Santa Cruz (Convento La Popa), and restored ruins of the convent dating from 1608 can be found here. In the church is the beautiful little image with a golden crown of the Virgin of La Candelaria, reputed as a deliverer from plague and a protector against pirates. The statue was blessed by the Pope on his visit in 1986. The Virgin's day is 2 February and for nine days before the feast thousands of people go up the hill by car, on foot, or on horseback. On the day itself people carry lighted candles as they go up the hill. There is an attractive bougainvillea-covered cloister with a well in the centre, and a museum with illuminated manuscripts, old maps, music books, relics and an image of the *Cabro de Oro* (golden goat) found by the Augustinians on the site, presumed to be an object of veneration of the indigenous people who previously inhabited the area. The name was bestowed on the hill because of an imagined likeness to a ship's poop deck.

Beaches → *For listings, see pages 36-43.*

Take a bus south from the Puerta del Reloj, taxi US$3, or walk to **Bocagrande**, where the beaches can be dirty in parts and often crowded. You will also be constantly hassled. The sea is a little dirty, though better if you go as far as the **Hilton** ⓘ *www.cartagena.hilton. com*, an excellent hotel at the end of the peninsula.

Marbella Beach is an alternative, just north of Las Bóvedas. This is the locals' beach, and therefore quieter than Bocagrande during the week and good for swimming, though subject at times to dangerous currents. The promontory beyond the airport is built up with high rises, including many well-known hotels which have their own access to the beach. City buses run to Los Morros and Las Américas conference centre, carrying on towards La Boquilla.

Bocachica Beach, on Tierrabomba island, isn't very clean either, and you may be hassled here too. Boats leave for Bocachica from Muelle Turístico. The departure point is the two-storey glass building halfway along, which also has some tourist information. The round trip can take up to two hours each way and costs about US$4 with the regular service, more if with private boats. *Ferry Dancing*, about half the price of the faster, luxury boats, carries dancing passengers. Boats taking in Bocachica and the San Fernando fortress include *Alcatraz*, which runs a daily trip from the Muelle Turístico. Alternatively, you can cross from Bocagrande; *lanchas* leave from near the Hilton hotel and go to **Punta Arena** beach on Tierrabomba.

Boats to the Islas del Rosario (see page 44) may stop at the **San Fernando** fortress on Tierrabomba island and **Playa Blanca** on the **Isla de Barú** for a couple of hours. Take food and water since these are expensive on Barú, a long thin island, with mostly fine white-sand beaches. The stopping place for tourist boats from Cartagena is Playa Blanca which is crowded in the mornings, but peaceful after the tour boats have left at around 1400. There are several fish restaurants on the beach, a growing number of upmarket places to stay and a few hammock and camping places (take repellent against sandflies if sleeping in a tent or *cabaña*). There have been reports of people drinking alcohol and then renting jetskis at Playa Blanca; keep your wits about you when swimming or snorkelling, as safety measures aren't always complied with. When taking boat trips be certain that you and the operator understand what you are paying for. You can arrange to be left and collected later, or you can try to catch an earlier boat on to Islas del Rosario or back to Cartagena with a boat that has dropped off people at the beach. ▸▸ *See Transport, page 43.*

Cartagena listings

For hotel and restaurant price codes and other relevant information, see pages 9-13.

⊙ Where to stay

Hotel prices rise for the high season, Nov-Mar and Jun-Jul. From 15 Dec to 31 Jan they can increase by as much as 50% (dates are not fixed and vary at each hotel). Hotels tend to be heavily booked right through to Mar.

Around the old city p27, map p28
Getsemaní and La Matuna

This area is very popular with travellers and has been smartened up, with many places to stay, eat and drink (lots of happy hour offers). Do not, however, walk alone late at night.
$$$ Monterrey, Paseo de los Mártires, Cra 8B, No 25-103, T650 3030, info@hotel monterrey.com.co (Hotel-Monterrey-Cartagena on Facebook). Just outside the old city walls and with a view onto the Puerta del Reloj, this hotel has rooms in simple colours with balconies, TV and hot water, internet. It also has a sunroof with pool and jacuzzi.
$$$-$$ Hostal Casa Baluarte, Media Luna, No 10-81, T664 2208, www.hostalcasa baluarte.com. A family-run, converted colonial house with a fine courtyard shaded by a mango tree and wrought-iron furniture, rocking chairs and hammocks in which to relax. Also offers massage. Can arrange tours to the Islas del Rosario and has laundry service. Rooms a little small.
$$ Marlin, C de la Media Luna, No 10-35, T664 3507, www.hotelmarlincartagena.com. Aquatic-themed hostel run by a friendly Colombian. Has a fine balcony looking onto the busy C de la Media Luna. Laundry service, free coffee, internet access, lockers, tours and bus tickets organized. Breakfast included. Recommended.
$$-$ Hostal La Casona, C Tripita y Media, Cra 10, No 31-32, T664 1301, www.hostal lacasonacartagena.com. Has a breezy

central courtyard and rooms for 1-6 people, some with private bath, with a/c or fan. Laundry service provided.
$$-$ Mamallena, C de la Media Luna, No 10-47, www.hostelmamallenacartagena. com. Rooms and dorms (some with a/c) in what was the **Holiday**. It's in same group as the **Mamallena** hostels in Panama, www. mamallena.com. Thorough information on boat travel to Panama and on local activities, offers day tours. There's a small kitchen, café, Wi-Fi, breakfast, tea and coffee included.
$$-$ Villa Colonial, C de las Maravillas 30-60, Getsemaní, T664 4996, hotelvilla colonial@hotmail.com. A safe, well-kept hostel run by a friendly family, English spoken, rooms are cheaper with fan. Arranges tours to Islas del Rosario. Its sister hotel, **Casa Villa Colonial**, C de la Media Luna No 10-89, T664 5421, www.casavilla colonial.net, is more upmarket (**$$$**) and is also recommended.
$ Casa Viena, C San Andrés, No 30-53, T664 6242, www.casaviena.com. Popular traveller hostel with very helpful staff who provide lots of information and sell tours and Brasilia bus tickets. Washing machine, TV room, book exchange, range of rooms from dorms to a few with private bath (**$$**), good value, security conscious. Enquire here for information about boats to Panama.
$ Familiar, C del Guerrero, No 29-66, off Media Luna, T664 2464. Fresh and bright, family-run hotel with rooms set around a colonnaded patio. Has a good noticeboard full of information, a laundry service and use of a kitchen. Friendly and recommended.

El Centro and San Diego
$$$$ Agua, C de Ayos, No 4-29, T664 9479, www.hotelagua.com.co. Exclusive, expensive, small boutique hotel, in colonial surroundings, quiet, with a very pleasant patio.
$$$$ Cartagena de Indias, C Vélez Daníes 33, No 4-39, T660 0133, www.movichhotels. com. A small hotel in a colonial building,

comfortable, luxury accommodation, good service, has a pool and a rooftop terrace with great view of the city.

$$$$ Casa de Pestagua, C Santo Domingo, No 33-63, T664 9510, www.casapestagua. com. Formerly home to the Conde de Pestagua, this historic house has been restored by architect Alvaro Barrera Herrera with great care. From the street it opens up into a magnificent colonnaded courtyard lined with enormous palm trees. Beyond is a swimming pool and spa, and on the top floor a sun terrace with jacuzzi and sea views.

$$$$ Casa San Agustín, C de la Universidad No 36-44, T681 0000, www.hotelcasasan agustin.com. A luxury boutique hotel in 3 historic buildings, combining the colonial architectural style with all modern facilities. Some rooms and suites have plunge pools and jacuzzis, all are spacious and elegant. It has the **Alma** restaurant and bar. Arranges trips to Islas del Rosario for guests.

$$$$ Charleston Santa Teresa, Cra 3, No 31-23, T664 9494, www.hotelcharleston santateresa.com. Formerly a convent, beautifully converted into a luxury hotel, stylish pool on the roof with great views of the colonial district and sea. Suites and standard rooms are in 2 wings, Colonial and Republican, 4 choices of restaurant, spa.

$$$$ El Marqués, C Nuestra Señora del Carmen, No 33-41, T664 7800, www.el marqueshotelboutique.com. Another house belonging to the Pestagua family. The central courtyard, dominated by a large crumbling wall of draping ivy, features giant birdcages, hanging bells and large palm trees. The rooms are crisp, white and have Wi-Fi and iPod docks. It has a Peruvian restaurant, a wine cellar and spa. Exquisite.

$$$$ La Passion, C Estanco del Tabaco, No 35-81, T664 8605, www.lapassion hotel.com. In the heart of the old city, this grand building brings the concept of the Marrakech boutique hotel to Latin America. Its French owners have trawled the globe in search of exquisite furnishings. A mixture of colonial and Republican-era

architecture, **La Passion** has cathedral-like rooms that provide modern, elegant and discreet comfort in the shape of plasma TVs, Wi-Fi and MP3 players. Breakfast is included in the price and served on the sublime roof terrace, next to the swimming pool. Also offers spa treatments including different massage and boat trips to nearby Islas del Rosario. Highly recommended.

$$$$ Santa Clara, C del Torno, No 39-29, T650 4700, www.sofitel.com. The French Sofitel group own this magnificently restored early 17th-century convent on the enchanting Plaza de San Diego. Rooms, however, are in a modern annex and most have a balcony looking onto a large swimming pool, invariably with views of the sea. Has 2 restaurants, a bar and a spa.

$$$$-$$$ Casa La Fe, Parque Fernández de Madrid, C 2a de Badillo, No 36-125, T664 0306, www.casalafe.com. A Republican-era house (c1930) on the delightful Parque Fernández de Madrid, the 14 en suite bedrooms of **Casa La Fe** have been restored by a British-Colombian team. It has a pool-jacuzzi on the roof and other services such as Wi-Fi, free bicycle use, and free breakfast served in a leafy patio. Organizes tours.

$$$ Hostal San Diego, C de las Bóvedas, No 39-120, T660 1433, www.hostalsandiego. com. Near the delightful Plaza San Diego, this colonial building with its salmon pink exterior has modern rooms which open out onto a tiled courtyard. A/c and Wi-Fi.

$$$ Las Tres Banderas, C Cochera de Hobo, No 38-66, T660 0160, www.hotel3 banderas.com. Another hotel in the bohemian district of San Diego, this old building is split over 2 breezy courtyards with water features. Popular, helpful owner, very pleasant, safe, quiet, good beds, spacious rooms, massage treatments, small patio. Price depends on standard of room and season. Free ferry transport to sister hotel on Isla de la Bomba; has another hotel at Manzanillo.

$$ Hotel El Viajero, C del Porvenir, No 35-68, piso 2, T664 3289, www.hotel elviajero.com. Ideally located in the centre of the old town, this 2nd-floor hostel is more practical than attractive. Organizes tours, has a/c, TV, Wi-Fi and access to a kitchen.

$$-$ El Viajero Hostel, C de los Siete Infantes 9-45, T660 2598, www.hostel cartagena.com. Member of the Uruguayan chain of hostels, spacious, with private rooms and dorms. A/c in some rooms, fan in others, breakfast included, free Wi-Fi and bar. Busy and popular, but a bit noisy.

Beaches *p35*
Bocagrande

$$$$ Capilla del Mar, Cra 1 No 8-12, T650 1501, www.capilladelmar.com. Resort hotel across the road from the beach, with swimming pool on the top floor and 2 restaurants, one a buffet, the other a sports bar.

$$$$ Hotel Caribe, Cra 1, No 2-87, T650 0155, www.hotelcaribe.com. Enormous Caribbean-style hotel, the first to be built in Cartagena, retaining some splendour of bygone years, with 2 newer annexes, a/c, beautiful grounds and a swimming pool. Expensive restaurant, has several bars overlooking the sea, various tour agencies and a dive shop.

$$$$ Playa Club, Av San Martín, No 4-87, T665 0552, www.hotelplayaclubcartagena. com. Some of the rooms are painted in lurid colours but are otherwise fine and it has an inviting pool and direct access to the beach. TV, a/c and breakfast included.

$$$$-$$$ Cartagena Millennium, Av San Martín, No 7-135, T665 8711, www.hotel cartagenamillennium.com. Has a range of different suites and spacious rooms at various prices. Chic and trendy, with minimalist decor, a small pool, restaurant serving typical and international food, a terrace bar and a lobby bar, good service.

$$$ Bahía, Cra 4 with C 4, T665 0316, www.hotelbahiacartagena.com. Has the feel of a 1950s hotel – it was opened in 1958 – but with mod cons such as Wi-Fi and safes in rooms. Discreet and quiet, with a fine pool and restaurant.

$$$ Charlotte, Av San Martín, No 7-126, T665 9298, www.hotelescharlotte.com. Stylishly designed in cool whites, comfortable rooms. Has a small pool, and Wi-Fi in the lobby. Smart restaurant serving Italian food. Recommended.

$$ Mary, Cra 3, No 6-53, T665 2833. Basic rooms but pleasant and friendly. A/c or fan.

Playa Blanca

$$$ Baruchica, Km 16, Vía Playa Blanca, on a private beach on Isla Barú, T317-657 1315. Ecolodge, B&B, owned and run by Olga Paulhiac, organic food, yoga available, evening cocktails, attentive service, delightful.

$ Hugo's Place, T310-716 1021. Hammocks with mosquito nets, fish meals served, camping.

Another place is **Mama Ruth** which is also recommended.

❼ Restaurants

There is a wide range of excellent, upmarket restaurants. **Crepes y Waffles** (6), **Jeno's Pizza** (4) and **Juan Valdez** (9) have outlets in the centre, Bocagrande and elsewhere. All restaurants are busy during high season, when reservations are recommended. At cafés try *patacón*, a round flat 'cake' made of green banana, mashed and baked; it's also available from street stalls in Parque del Centenario in the early morning. At restaurants ask for *sancocho*, the local soup of the day of vegetables and fish or meat. Also try *obleas* for a snack, biscuits with jam, cream cheese or caramel fudge (*arequipe*), and *buñuelos*, deep-fried cheese dough balls. Fruit juices are fresh, tasty and cheap in Cartagena: a good place is on the Paseo de los Pegasos (Av Blas de Lezo) from the many stalls alongside the boats.

The city's fortifications *p27*

$$$ Club de Pesca, San Sebastián de Pastelillo fort, Manga Island, T660 4594, www.clubdepesca.com. Wonderful setting, perhaps the most famous fish and seafood restaurant in Cartagena, though expensive. Warmly recommended.

Around the old city *p27, map p28*
Getsemaní and La Matuna

With spiralling property prices Getsemaní is undergoing the same gentrification treatment as Centro and San Diego, which is reflected in the number of smart restaurants opening up in the area.

$$ La Casa de Socorro, C Larga, No 8B-112, T664 4658, www.restaurantelacasade socorro.com. This seafood restaurant is popular with locals and does very good *bandejas de pescado* and *arroz con camarones*. Take note that there are 2 rival restaurants of the same name on the same street. This one is the original. Friendly and recommended.

$$-$ La Cocina de Pepina, Callejón Vargas, No 9A-6, T664 2944. Daily 1200-1600. A restaurant serving Colombian Caribbean cuisine, run by established chef and cookbook author María Josefina Yances Guerra.

$$-$ Lunarossa, C de la Media Luna y San Andrés. Italian restaurant and bar serving thin-crust pizza, pasta and other dishes.

$ Café Lunático, C Media Luna 10-81, T301-740 0642 (next door to Hostal Casa Baluarte). Interesting café with fresh juices, local and Indian dishes. Also sells weavings and blankets.

$ El Coroncoro, C Tripita y Media, No 31-28. More typical of the area, very popular at lunchtime with locals. It's atmospheric and offers *menús del día* from US$2.75; main dishes from US$5.50, breakfasts US$3.75.

$ Este es el punto, C San Andrés No 30-35. Another popular restaurant, *comida corriente* at lunchtime, US$3.50, also serves breakfast.

El Centro and San Diego

Plaza San Diego has several good restaurants serving a variety of international cuisine.

$$$-$$ Donde Olano, C Santo Domingo, No 33-08, e Inquisición, T664 7099, www. dondeolanorestaurante.blogspot.co.uk. Art deco restaurant serving French and Creole cuisine in a cosy atmosphere. Try their fantastic seafood platter, *Tentaciones de Zeus*. Well worth the price.

$$ Balkoon, C de Tumbamuertos, No 38-85, p 2 (above Zebra). Small restaurant with a nice balcony overlooking the Plaza de San Diego. Good atmosphere and good views.

$$ Bistro, C de los Ayos, No 4-46. German-run restaurant with a relaxed atmosphere, closed Sun. Sofas, music, Colombian and European menu at reasonable prices, German bakery. Recommended.

$$ Juan del Mar, Plaza San Diego, No 8-18. Offers 2 restaurants in one: expensive seafood is served inside, while fine thin-crust pizzas are available outside, though you are likely to be harassed by street hawkers.

$$ Oh! La La, C de los Ayos, No 4-50. Café/restaurant serving good French and Colombian food. Next door are Jugoso juice bar and El Gallinero for ice creams, yoghurts and snacks.

$$ Teppanyaki, Plaza San Diego, No 8-28. Serves sushi and Thai food in smart surroundings.

$$ Zebra, Plaza San Diego, No 8-34. Café with wide selection of coffees, hot sandwiches and African dishes.

$$-$ Casa Suiza, C de la Soledad No 5-38. For breakfast, lunch such as lasagne, salads, cheeses dishes; also does take-away, Wi-Fi.

$$-$ La Mulata, C Quero, No 9-58. A popular lunchtime venue with locals, you get a selection of set menu dishes. Try the excellent seafood casserole and coconut lemonade. Wi-Fi.

$$ Perú Fusión, C de los Ayos, No 4-42. Good-value Peruvian-style food, including *ceviches*.

$ La Esquina del Pan de Bono, San Agustín Chiquito No 35-78, opposite Plazoleta San Agustín. Breads, *empanadas, pasteles* and juices, popular for a quick snack.

$ Pizza en el parque, C 2a de Badillo, No 36-153. This small restaurant serves delicious pizzas with some interesting flavours (pear and apple) which you can munch on while enjoying the delightful atmosphere of Parque Fernández de Madrid.

Beaches *p35*
There are good fish dishes in La Boquilla.

Bocagrande
$$$ Ranchería's, Av 1A, No 8-86.
Serves mainly seafood and meats in
thatched huts just off the beach.
$$$-$$ Arabe, Cra 3A, No 8-83, T665
4365. Upmarket Arab restaurant serving
tagines, etc. A/c, indoor seating or pleasant
outdoor garden.
$$$-$$ Carbón de Palo, Av San Martín,
No 6-40. Steak heaven (and other dishes),
cooked on an outdoor *parrilla*.
$ La Fonda Antioqueña, Cra 2, No 6-164.
Traditional Colombian food served in a
nice atmosphere.

⒪ Bars and clubs

Cartagena boasts a lively dance scene and the
atmosphere in the city after dark is addictive.
Any one of the cafés next to the Santo
Domingo church is a great place for a drink.

Around the old city *p27, map p28*
Many of the hotels have evening
entertainment and can arrange *chiva*
(brightly coloured local bus) tours, usually
with free drinks and live music on the bus.
  There are good local nightclubs in
Bocagrande eg **La Escollera**, Cra 1, next to El
Pueblito shopping centre, with other places
nearby including spontaneous musical
groups on or near the beach most evenings.
  Most places don't get going until after
2400, though the Cuban bar **Donde Fidel**, on
Portal de los Dulces, and **Café Havana**, on C de
la Media Luna in Getsemaní (see below) start
a little earlier and are highly recommended if
you want to hear Cuban salsa. The former is
open during the daytime and the atmosphere
is good even early on. C del Arsenal hosts
many clubs and you will probably wind up
there if you are really giving the city's nightlife
a go. Most bars play crossover music.
Café del Mar, Baluarte de Santo Domingo,
El Centro. The place to go at sundown,

where, surrounded by ancient canons, you
can watch the sun set over the bay. Highly
recommended, but very popular. Get here
early to get a seat for the sundowners.
Café Havana, C de la Media Luna y C
del Guerrero, T310-610 2324, www.cafe
havanacartagena.com. Thu-Sat and
holidays 2030-0400. A fantastic Cuban
bar and restaurant, which feels like it
has been transported from Havana
brick by brick. The walls are festooned
with black-and-white portraits of Cuban
salsa stars and it has live bands playing
most nights. Note that it doesn't take
credit cards. Highly recommended.
Mister Babilla, C Larga. A popular,
exclusive bar. Take something warm with
you – they really like to blast the a/c here.
Quiebra Canto, C Media Luna at Parque
Centenario, next to **Hotel Monterrey**,
Getsemaní. The best place for salsa.
Nice atmosphere, free admission.
Tu Candela, Portal de los Dulces, next
door to Donde Fidel. Open from 2000.

Gay bars
Studio 54, C Larga, No 8B-24, Getsemaní.

☻ Entertainment

Cartagena *p24, map p28*
Cinema
There are many cinemas in Cartagena.
In Bocagrande there is one in the **Centro
Comercial Bocagrande**, Cra 2, No 8-146,
T665 5024. Others are in the **Centro
Comercial Paseo de la Castellana** at
C 30, No 30-31, and in **Centro Comercial
La Plazuela**, Diag 31, No 71-136.

Dance
El Colegio del Cuerpo, Campus Universidad
Jorge Tadeo Lozano, Módulo 6, Km 13, Anillo
Vial Zona Norte, T665 4081, www.elcolegio
delcuerpo.org. A classical dance studio
that works with children from Cartagena's
slums. They perform internationally and
occasionally in Cartagena.

🎉 Festivals

Cartagena *p24, map p28*
Mid-Jan Festival Internacional de Música, www.cartagenamusicfestival.com. Classical music festival with associated education programme for young musicians.
End-Jan Hay Festival Cartagena, www.hayfestival.com. Franchise of the famous UK literary festival, with internationally renowned writers.
End-Jan Cartagena de Indias Jazz Fest, www.cartagenadeindiasjazzfest.com.
Jan-Feb La Candelaria, religious processions and horse parades (see La Popa, page 34).
2nd week of Mar International Film Festival, www.ficcifestival.com. The longest running festival of its kind in Latin America. Although mainly Spanish American films are featured, the US, Canada and European countries are represented in the week-long showings.
1 Jun Celebrations commemorating the Foundation of Cartagena.
2nd week of Nov Independence celebrations: masked people in fancy dress dance to the sound of *maracas* and drums. There are beauty contests, battles of flowers and general mayhem.

🛍 Shopping

Cartagena *p24, map p28*
Galería Cano, Plaza Bolívar No 33-20, www.galeriacano.com.co (and at the airport and Hotel Santa Clara), has excellent reproductions of pre-Columbian designs. Pricey antiques can be bought in C Santo Domingo and there are a number of jewellery shops near Plaza de Bolívar in Centro, which specialize in emeralds.

The handicraft shops in the Plaza de las Bóvedas (see page 33) have the best selection in town but tend to be expensive–cruise ship passengers are brought here. Woollen *blusas* are good value; try the Tropicano in Pierino Gallo building in Bocagrande. Also in this building are reputable jewellery shops.

Abaco, C de la Iglesia with C Mantilla, No 3-86, T664 8338, www.abacolibros.com. A bookshop and popular hangout for local writers and poets. Delightful atmosphere and a café serving juices and snacks.
Centro Comercial Getsemaní, C Larga between San Juan and Plaza de la Independencia. A large shopping centre. Good *artesanías* in the grounds of the convent.
El Centavo Menos, C Román, No 5-08, Plaza de la Proclamación. Good selection of Colombian handicrafts.
Exito, Escallón y del Boquete. A supermarket, with a/c and cafeteria.
H Stern, Pierino Gallo shopping centre and at the **Hilton Hotel**. Jewellery shop.
Librería Nacional, C 2 de Badillo, No 36-27, T664 1448, www.librerianacional.com. A good bookshop with large stock.
Santo Domingo, C Santo Domingo, No 3-34. Recommended for jewellery.
Upalema, C San Juan de Dios, No 3-99, www.upalema.com. A good selection of handicrafts.

Markets
The main market is to the southeast of the old city near La Popa off Av Pedro de Heredia (**Mercado Bazurto**). Good bargains in the **La Matuna** market, open daily including Sun.

🎯 What to do

Cartagena *p24, map p28*
City tours
Many agencies, hotels and hostels offer them, US$22. There is also a hop-on, hop-off city sightseeing bus tour. A party tour on a *chiva* bus costs US$19.50. **Horse-drawn carriages** can be hired for for a trip around the walled city from Puerta del Reloj, about US$20 for up to 4 people. Or from opposite Hotel El Dorado, Av San Martín, in Bocagrande, to ride into town at night (romantic but a rather short ride). You can also rent **bicycles** for riding the city streets, eg **Cartagena de Indias Bike Rental**, Estrella

No 4-34, and C San Pedro Mártir 1086,
T660 5156, www.cartagenadeindiasbike
rental.com, US$2.75 per hr.

Diving

Discounts are sometimes available if you
book via the hotels. There is a recompression
chamber at the naval hospital in Bocagrande.
Cultura del Mar, C del Pozo, No 25-95,
Getsemaní, T664 9312. Run by a team of
young, well-informed Colombians. Diving,
snorkelling and tours to Islas del Rosario,
English spoken, environmentally responsible.
Diving Planet, C Estanco del Aguardiente,
No 5-94, T664 2171, www.divingplanet.org.
PADI training courses, PADI e-learning,
snorkelling trips, English spoken. Associated
hotel in Cartagena, **Puertas de Cartagena**,
www.hotelpuertasdecartagena.com.
La Tortuga Dive Shop, Edif Marina del Rey,
C 1, No 2-23, loc 4, Av del Retorno, El Laguito,
Bocagrande, T665 6994/5, www.tortuga
dive.com. Fast boat, which allows for
trips to Isla Barú as well as Los Rosarios.

Football

Estadio de Futbol Pedro de Heredia,
Villa Olímpica, south of the city. Games
are infrequent.

Language schools

Nueva Lengua School, www.nueva
lengua. com. Offers courses ranging
from ½-day schedules to a scheme that
arranges volunteer jobs. There are even
Spanish courses combined with dance,
music, adventure, kitesurfing or diving.

Tour operators

Aventure Colombia, C del Santísimo,
No 8-55, T664 8500, T314-588 2378,
www.aventurecolombia.com. Also with
a branch in Bogotá. The only tour organizer
of its kind in Cartagena, French/Colombian-
run, offering alternative tours across
Colombia, local and national activities and
expeditions, working (wherever possible)
with local and indigenous groups. The

focus is on ecotourism and trekking, also
organizes boat trips. Highly recommended.
Ocean & Land, Cra 2, No 4-15, Edif Antillas,
Bocagrande, T665 727, oceanlandtours_
cartagena@hotmail.com. Organizes city
tours, rumbas in *chivas* (brightly coloured
local buses) and other local activities.

Yachting

Club Náutico, Av Miramar No 19-50,
on Manga Island across the Puente
Román, T660 4863, www.clubnautico
cartagena.com. Good for opportunities
to charter, crew or for finding a lift to
other parts of the Caribbean.

⊖ Transport

Cartagena *p24, map p28*
Air
There are direct flights daily to major
Colombian cities and to smaller places
in the north of the country, as well as
international flights direct to **Lauderdale**,
Miami, **New York** and **Panama**. From
Dec to Mar flights can be overbooked,
so turn up at the airport early.
　　Airline offices Avianca, C del
Arzobispado, No 34-52, T664 7376, Mon-Fri
0800-1200, 1400-1800, Sat 0800-1300,
Av Venezuela 33, No 8B-05, Edif City Bank,
loc B2, T664 7822, also in Bocagrande, C 7,
No 7-17, L 7, T665 0287 and at the airport,
T666 1175. **Copa**, Av San Martín Cra 2,
No 10-54, Edif Sky II Bolívar (Bocagrade),
T6650428, Mon-Fri 0800-1800, Sat 0900-
1300. **EasyFly**, T693 0400 **LAN**, Carrera 3
No 4 – 21 local 1. **Viva Colombia**, T642 4989.

Bus
Several bus companies run to **Barranquilla**,
every 15 mins, 2-3 hrs, US$7-8; **Berlinastur**
minibus service from Av 1, No 65-129,
Crespo, T318-724 2424. *Colectivos* for
Barranquilla leave from C 70, Barrio Crespo,
every 2 hrs, US$14, centre-to-centre
service. To **Santa Marta**, hourly, US$18,
4 hrs. Few buses go direct to Santa Marta

from Cartagena, most stop in Barranquilla. To/from **Bogotá** via Barranquilla and Bucaramanga, 16 a day, 21-28 hrs (depending on number of checkpoints), US$72-75, several companies. To **Medellín** 665 km, US$55-70, more or less hourly from 0530, 13-16 hrs. Book early (2 days in advance at holiday times). The road is paved throughout, but in poor condition. To **Magangué** on the Magdalena US$20, 4 hrs with Brasilia; to **Mompós**, see page 45. To **Riohacha**, US$24. Bus to **Maicao** on Venezuelan border, every hour 0500-1200, 2 in the evening, 12 hrs, US$30, with Brasilia.

Car hire
Several of the bigger hotels have car rental offices in their foyers, such as Bechs, Hotel Bahía, Bocagrande, C 4, No 3-59, local 1, T665 6314. There are car rental companies in Edif Torremolinos, Av San Martín: **International Car Rentals**, T665 5399; **National**, T665 3336; and on Av San Martín: **Budget**, No 13-37 L-3, T655 1848, **Trans**, No 11-67, Edif Tulipana L-5, T665 2427. At the airport, try **Car y Rental** of 103, T666 4112.

Sea
Boats go from Cartagena to the San Blas Islands (**Panama**); the journey takes 5 days in all, 2 sailing to the archipelago and 3 touring the San Blas islands. Trips usually end at Puerto Lindo on the mainland, from where you can continue to Colón and thence to Panama City. The fare, about US$550 in 2013, includes food and passport stamps. Some boats are cheaper, but you get what you pay for.

Take your time before choosing a boat. Some captains are irresponsible and unreliable. The journey is cramped so it's best to get on with the captain. There are many notices in hostels in Getsemaní advertising this trip, for example in **Casa Viena** and **Mamallena**. Also **Sailing Koala**, T300-805 1816, www.sailingkoala.com, which offers a trip to San Blas and Panama.

Note On the street, do not be tempted by offers of jobs or passages

onboard a ship. Jobs should have full documentation from the Seamen's Union office and passages should only be bought at a recognized shipping agency.

Beaches *p35*
There are 3 ways of getting to **Playa Blanca**. The most common is to take a bus from the centre to **Pasacaballo**, US$1. From there take a 5-min ferry over the Río Magdalena, US$0.55. Then take a motortaxi to Playa Blanca via **Santa Ana** (45 mins), US$4.50-5.50. Do not give money or gifts to children dancing on the roadway. Alternatively, fast boats to Playa Blanca leave **Bazurto** market, near La Popa, from 0700-0930 daily, US$13.75 one way. Public boats cost US$5.50-8.50. Neither the area nor the boats are particularly safe and boatmen can be persistent. Be sure to pay the captain and not his 'helpers' and arrange a return pick-up time. There are also touristy, expensive boats from the tourist dock (*Muelle Turístico*) at 0830 which stop at Playa Blanca as part of a tour, US$33.

❶ Directory

Cartagena *p24, map p28*
Banks There are many ATMs, the most convenient are in the Plaza de la Aduana, the banks in La Matuna (across from Parque del Centenario) and the **Exito** supermarket, Escallón y Boquete. In Bocagrande a number of banks can be found around Av San Martín y C 8. Never change money on the street under any circumstances. There are *cambios* in the arcade at Torre Reloj and adjoining streets (Carretas, Manuel Román y Pico, Colegio). **Embassies and consulates** For your country's embassy or consulates in Colombia, see http://embassy.goabroad.com. **Immigration** Migración Colombia: Cra 20B, No 29-18, T666 3092, open 0800-1200, 1400-1700. **Medical services** Hospital Bocagrande, C 5/Cra 6, Bocagrande, T650 2800, www.nhbg.com.co.

Around Cartagena

Cartagena is surrounded on almost all sides by water and travellers will be drawn to the city's sparkling Caribbean coast. Islas del Rosario and Islas San Bernardo are glistening examples of what a tropical paradise should look like. To the northeast of Cartagena, the coastline is characterized by *ciénagas* (mangrove swamps), such as the Ciénaga La Caimanera, which provide plenty of opportunities to observe the wildlife that exists in these remarkable ecosystems. A few kilometres further on is the Volcán del Totumo, an extraordinary crater-like mud hole where bathers can wallow before washing off in the nearby *ciénaga*.

Volcán del Totumo → *For listings, see pages 51-56.*

Along the coast north of Cartagena, at La Boquilla, is the Ciénaga la Caimanera, a labyrinth of mangrove swamps full of wildlife. Canoe trips can be made to explore these (motorboats are not allowed). Local guides cost US$15 per person, and they will catch oysters for you to eat. Further north is **Galerazamba**; there is no accommodation but good local food. Nearby is the clay bath of **Volcán del Totumo** ① *entry to the cone US$2.50, children US$1.75, the unusual experience will cost you a further US$2.50 for various services (massage, photo, etc) and you wash off in the nearby Ciénaga*, in beautiful surroundings. Climb up steep steps to the lip of the 20-m-high crater and slip into the grey cauldron of mud, which is a comfortable temperature. The crater is about 10 m across and reputed to be over 500 m deep.

To get there, catch a bus from Cartagena bus terminal to the turn-off (US$7.50, 45 km), then take a mototaxi to the crater (US$ 1.30, 10 minutes). Taking a tour from Cartagena may cost more but will save a lot of time. Tours to the volcano last about six hours and cost between US$2 and US$40 depending on what is included (with or without lunch, trip to Manzanillo beach, etc). This has become a very popular excursion and the bath may be very busy.

Islas del Rosario → *For listings, see pages 51-56.*

The Parque Nacional Corales del Rosario y San Bernardo embraces the archipelago of Rosario (a group of 30 coral islets, 45 km southwest of the Bay of Cartagena), the mangrove coast of the long island of Barú to its furthest tip (see above) and the Islas de San Bernardo (see under Tolú, below). **Isla Grande** and some of the smaller islets are easily accessible for day trippers and those who wish to stay in one of the hotels. Permits are needed for the rest; entrance fee US$3. These picture-postcard islands, low lying and densely vegetated, with narrow strips of fine sand beaches, form part of a coral reef. **Rosario** (the largest and best conserved) and **Tesoro** both have small lakes, some of which connect to the sea, and

Mud volcanoes

The Caribbean coast is peppered with several geological curiosities popularly known as 'mud volcanoes'. These large mud pools are believed to be the result of underground oil and gas deposits, which combine with water, forcing the mud to ooze to the surface. Often they form conical mounds, hence the name. Many of these pools can be found between the Gulf of Urabá and Santa Marta. Turbo has several in its proximity (Rodosalín, El Alto de Mulatos and Caucal), as does San Pedro de Urabá. The Volcán de Totumo is a popular day

trip from Cartagena, but the pick of the bunch is Arboletes, where an enormous 30-m-wide lake has formed a stone's throw from the beach.

Wallowing in the grey-black mud is a strange experience. It's impossible to sink and attempts to swim are about as worthwhile as trying to battle your way across a vat of treacle. When you have had enough, clamber out and join the line of mud-caked figures waddling down to the Caribbean for a wash and a swim. The stuff is reportedly an excellent exfoliant and does wonders for the skin and hair.

many of the smaller islets are privately owned. There is a profusion of aquatic and birdlife here and the **San Martín de Pajarales Aquarium** (**Oceanario**) ① *US$10*, is worth visiting. Look out for the huge catfish but note that the price of entry is not included in boat fares. The island has access to some of the best coral reefs in the archipelago and diving and snorkelling are available. ▸▸ *See What to do, page 54.*

Travel agencies and the hotels offer excursions from the Muelle Turístico, leaving 0700-0900 and returning 1600-1700, costing from around US$45 (free if staying at one of the hotels), lunch included. Overnight trips can be arranged through agencies, but they are overpriced. Note that there is an additional 'port tax' of US$6 payable at the entrance to the Muelle or on the boat. Book in advance. For five or more people, try hiring your own boat for the day and bargain your price. This way you get to see what you want in the time available. The tour boats leave you with plenty of time with the beach vendors. For the cheapest rates, buy tickets from the boat owners (make sure they are the boat owners!) at the dockside, but they may already be booked up.

If you wish to enjoy the islands at your leisure there are several hotels. ▸▸ *See Where to stay, page 51.*

Mompós → *For listings, see pages 51-56.*

The highway south towards Medellín goes through **Turbaco**, 24 km (there's a botanical garden 1.5 km before the village on the left, Tuesday-Sunday 0900-1600), **Malagana**, 60 km, **San Jacinto**, known for its cumbia music using gaitas and local craft work (hand-woven hammocks) and **El Carmen de Bolívar**, 125 km. A road runs east from the highway at El Bongo to **Magangué**, on the western loop of the Río Magdalena. It is the port for the savannas of Bolívar. From here boats go to La Bodega where you pick up the road again for the small town of **Mompós** (also spelt Mompox) on an island in the middle of the Río Magadalena. Thanks to a geographical anomaly, the town (officially known as Santa Cruz de Mompós) retains much the same atmosphere you might have experienced had you visited in the early 20th century.

Arriving in Mompós

To reach Mompós from Cartagena there are three options, all involving a short river journey from Magangué to La Bodega: a through bus; a bus to Magangué, then a ferry or *chalupa* (motorized canoe), followed by *colectivo* from La Bodega; lastly, a *colectivo* direct from your hotel. There is also transport from Barranquilla, Santa Marta and Valledupar, as well as from the south. ▶▶ *See Transport, page 54.*

Places in Mompós

The grand old Magdalena River splits in two just before Mompós. When the town was founded in 1540, the Mompós branch of the river was the main tributary and it became a major staging port for travellers and merchandise going to the interior. But at the beginning of the 20th century it silted up with mud and became unnavigable for large boats, so traffic was diverted to the Brazo de Lobo. As a result, Mompós became a backwater and it has remained practically untouched ever since.

In 1995 UNESCO declared it a World Heritage Site for the quality of its colonial architecture and its fine churches, and it was the setting for the film adaptation of Gabriel García Márquez's *Chronicle of a Death Foretold* (1987).

Today, in the evenings, as the sweltering heat begins to lessen and the bats start to swoop from the eaves of the whitewashed houses, locals carry their rocking chairs out

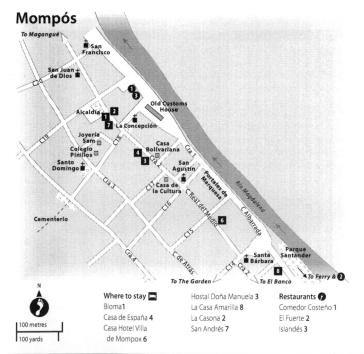

Mompós

Where to stay 🛏
Bioma 1
Casa de España 4
Casa Hotel Villa
   de Mompox 6
Hostal Doña Manuela 3
La Casa Amarilla 8
La Casona 2
San Andrés 7

Restaurants 🍴
Comedor Costeño 1
El Fuerte 2
Islandés 3

100 metres
100 yards

onto the streets to chat with neighbours and watch the world go by. Cars are rare here, the main forms of transport are bicycle, moped, auto-rickshaw – or on foot.

Part of Mompós' charm lies in the fact that it is still quite difficult to reach – all journeys include a combination of bus, motorized canoe or ferry and car. Plans are afoot to improve transport connections, but with luck, these won't detract from its languid charm.

The churches demonstrate the colonial origins of the town; five of the six are close to the centre. The church of **San Francisco** is probably the oldest, dating from the end of the 16th century, with an interesting interior. **Santa Bárbara**, on Calle 14 by the river, has a unique octagonal Moorish tower and balcony. **San Juan de Dios**, **La Concepción**, **Santo Domingo** and **San Agustín** are all worth visiting. You may have to ask around for the key to see inside; they are not normally open except during Mass. Guides who approach you on the street can gain access to all the buildings (tours of the city on foot or motortaxi cost US$6 per hour). In the **Claustro de San Agustín** is a workshop where youngsters are taught local skills. Among other old buildings are the **Casa de Gobierno**, once a home of the Jesuits and now the Alcaldía, and the **Colegio Pinillos**. Facing the river, on the Albarrada, are the old customs house and the mansions of Spanish merchants, for instance the Portales La Marquesa. Rows of well-preserved buildings, some with balconies, have served as a backdrop in many Colombian films. The cemetery is of considerable historical interest; on one side of the central avenue lie the Conservatives, on the other the Liberals. This political division of the town continued down Calle 18, running from the cemetery to the river. Try to visit the cemetery on the Wednesday of **Semana Santa** when it is illuminated by thousands of candles lit by the locals to honour the dead. On Calle 14, opposite Carrera 4, is a garden open to visitors (usually) with trees and flowering plants. The town is well known in Colombia for hand-worked gold and silver jewellery, especially filigree, as well as its wicker rocking chairs.

Mompós was particularly dear to Simón Bolívar, as it was the site of one of the greatest victories in his campaign to expel the Spanish from South America. "If to Caracas I owe my life, then to Mompós I owe my glory," he said (a monument outside the Alcaldía proclaims this). He stayed in what is now called the **Museo Cultural Casa Bolivariana** ① *C del Medio y 17, no regular opening hours*, which houses memorabilia of his times and also has some religious art exhibits. The **Casa de la Cultura** is a particularly interesting colonial building and home of the local Academy of History.

Boat trips ① *3-4 hrs, US$14-17*, can be taken along the Río Magdalena and into the surrounding wetlands, which provide excellent opportunities for birdwatching. In the early morning or at dusk, you can walk along the river bank to look for birds, or in the afternoon. Cross the river on the small ferry from beyond the Parque Santander, US$0.50. Walk a little way up the track to a where it meets another track. Turn sharp right and look for birds in the wet areas beyond the cattle pens. Beware of dogs. You can't walk directly along the riverbank as it's fenced.

Ferocious mosquitoes and the odd bat are a nuisance after dusk; take insect repellent and wear long sleeves.

Just a few years ago, the area south of Cartagena was a no-go zone. The road between Cartagena and Medellín was the scene of frequent kidnappings by guerrillas who would perform raids on passing traffic and quickly abscond into the region's network of densely vegetated hills. Today it's a different story and locals no longer sweat before making what was once a perilous journey. A word of warning, however: drug smuggling is still very active in the area near the Panama border. Towns such as Sincelejo and Montería are fine to pass through but we advise against staying there too long. It is now considered reasonably safe to travel at night between Cartagena and Medellín.

The improvement in security also means that this area, rich in culture and natural wonders, has opened up to tourism. Due south is Tolú, gateway to the coral islands of San Bernardo (part of the Corales de Rosario and San Bernardo National Park), while further along the coast is Arboletes, location of the largest mud volcano in the area. Further still is Turbo, a rough frontier town from where boats can be caught to the emerald green coastline of the Darién.

Tolú

Tolú, 35 km northwest of Sincelejo, on the coast, is a fast developing holiday town popular with Colombians and, increasingly, foreign tourists attracted by visits to the offshore islands and diving. Along the *malecón* (promenade), there are plenty of bars and restaurants. A distinctive feature of the town are the bicycle rickshaws armed with loud sound-systems blasting out *vallenato*, salsa and reggaeton. The rickshaw drivers spend much of their time trying to outdo each other with the volume of their music. Tolú can also be reached more directly from Cartagena, through **San Onofre**, then, after 46 km from San Onofre, turn right for Tolú. Continue straight on from Toluviejo for 20 km to Sincelejo.

A good boat trip from Tolú is to the beautiful beaches of Múcura island or Tintipán in the **Islas de San Bernardo**, about US$25, 45 minutes. Trips to the mangrove lagoons are also recommended. **Club Náutico Maradentro** ① *www.clubnauticomaradentro.com*, runs daily boats to the San Bernardo Islands at 0830, returning at 1230, which cost US$20 for a return trip. **Isla Múcura** has a number of shacks serving seafood, including excellent barbecued lobster. The beach is of fine white sand with beautiful, clear water. Unfortunately, with several launches converging on the island at the same time, it can get crowded and the number of beach vendors can detract from the beauty of the place. There is a charge for everything, including sitting at a table. To enjoy the islands at your leisure, it is better to stay overnight. It's also possible to reach the island from Cartagena, if you have a reservation at **Punta Faro** (one hour 45 minutes by boat, transfer included in the cost of accommodation). ▸▸ *See Where to stay and What to do, pages 52 and 54.*

There are two mud volcanoes to visit. The closest one is in **San Antero**, 30 minutes' drive from Tolú; the other is in San Bernardo del Viento (1¼ hours, see below). Both make good day trips. A six-hour tour to San Antero, including other sites of interest and lunch, costs US$55.

There are, perhaps surprisingly, good beaches at **Coveñas**, 20 km further southwest, the terminal of the oil pipeline from the oilfields in the Venezuelan border area. Coveñas is essentially a 5-km-long stretch of road peppered with *cabañas* and hotels. During high season (Easter, Christmas to mid-January, June and July) it is very popular with Colombians eager to hit the beach and party. To get there, take a bus or *colectivo* from Tolú.

Further along the coast, turning right 18 km southwest of Coveñas at Lorica is **San Bernardo del Viento** from where launches can be arranged to **Isla Fuerte**, an unspoilt coral island with fine beaches and simple places to stay. It's a good place to dive, but there are very limited facilities on the island. Enquire at travel agencies in Medellín and elsewhere for inclusive trips or negotiate in San Bernardo.

Arboletes

Southwest of Tolú is the unremarkable town of Arboletes which nonetheless has an extraordinary attraction: the largest mud volcano in the area. Dipping into this swimming pool-sized mud bath is a surreal experience – like swimming in treacle. It's also very good for your skin. You can wash the mud off in the sea by walking to the beach 100 m below. Arboletes is also a convenient stopover on the way to Turbo and the Darién coast.

The **Volcán de Lodo** is a 15-minute walk from town on the road to Montería or a two-minute taxi ride (US$7 return; the driver will wait for you while you bathe). A mototaxi costs US$1.50. There is a small restaurant and changing rooms (US$ 0.50), plus a locker room (US$1 per bag) and showers (US$0.50).

Turbo

At the mouth of the Gulf of Urabá is the port of Turbo: a hot, rough, frontier community with a lawless feel about it. It is a centre for banana cultivation. There is little reason to stop here except to catch a boat to Capurganá and the Panamanian border.

Darién Gap

The Darién Gap has long held a special place in travellers' lore as the ultimate adventure – and for good reason. This thin stretch of land, just 50 km wide and 160 km long, which links Central and South America, has some of the densest tropical jungle in the world – so dense that to date neither the Panamanians nor the Colombians have succeeded in building a road across. There are no roads of any kind, the only inland routes are by boat or on foot. At present, the Pan-American Highway from Canada to Tierra del Fuego in Chile stops at Yaviza in Panama, 60 km short of the frontier, and begins again 27 km west of Barranquillita, well into Colombia. The Darién is home to an incredible profusion of flora and fauna, as well as indigenous tribes who rarely see foreigners.

The trek across the Darién is held in high regard by adventurers but we strongly advise against it, not simply because it is easy (and fatal) to get lost, but also because bona fide travellers are not welcome (indigenous communities still living in Darién have never truly accepted trekkers passing through) and this area still has a heavy guerrilla presence. The Colombian government's successes against the FARC have pushed them to the extremes of the country. Those trafficking drugs from South to North America have found the density of the jungle a useful protection for running consignments. Both FARC and ELN guerrilla groups have infiltrated the region and paramilitaries regard this as a threat to their land. As a result this has become a war zone, virtually deserted now by police and the military, and it is a hostile environment for any tourist. For the moment only the foolhardy will attempt the land crossing. However, the Caribbean coastline, heavily patrolled by Colombian and Panamanian forces, is safe, though you should exercise caution if venturing into the forest beyond.

Acandí

Acandí is a small fishing village on the Caribbean side of the Darién. It has a spectacular, forest-fringed bay with turquoise waters. To the south are other bays and villages, such as **San Francisco**. From March to June, thousands of leatherback turtles come here to lay their eggs. There are several cheap *residencias* to stay in.

Capurganá

For many years, Capurganá and neighbouring Sapzurro (see below) have been among the best-kept secrets in Colombia. In this most isolated of Colombia's corners, a glistening, untouched shoreline of crystal waters and coral reefs backs onto quiet little villages where, at night, if you listen carefully, you can hear the howler monkeys calling to each other in the jungle-clad hills behind.

Capurganá has developed into a resort popular with affluent Colombians and is increasingly visited by foreigners, despite being somewhat difficult or expensive to get to. It is a quiet place: there are no banks or ATMs, nor are there any cars, just a couple of motorbikes. Taxi rides are provided by horse and carts, and someone has had the ingenious idea of attaching modified plastic seats.

There are two beaches in the village. **La Caleta** is at the northern end, beyond the pontoon, and is protected by a barrier reef, has golden sand and is the best for swimming. There are a couple of restaurants and several hotels and *cabañas* here. **Playa de los Pescadores**, south of the village, is fringed by palm and almond trees but has disappointing grey sand and is more pebbly. Ask the fishermen about fishing trips from here in rowing boats.

Around Capurganá

Several half- and full-day trips can be made by launch to neighbouring beaches. **Aguacate** is a beautiful bay with clear, aquamarine water and a small beach. There is a rocky promontory with a blowhole and what locals call '*La Piscina*', a natural jacuzzi amongst the rocks which you can lower yourself into using a rope. There is also a small restaurant serving fried fish for US$7. Aguacate has good snorkelling, but **Playa Soledad** is perhaps the most attractive beach in the area and was recently used as the location for a Colombian reality TV programme. The beach is white sand and fringed by palms. A return trip by launch boat costs US$15 per person, minimum five people. You can also walk to Aguacate, 1½ hours along the coast, though not to Playa Soledad. Note that it can be difficult to obtain a return by launch if you walk.

A delightful half-day excursion is to **El Cielo** ① *0600-1700, US$1.75; 40-min walk, take flip flops or waterproof boots for crossing a stream several times*, a small waterfall in the jungle. Take the path to the left of the airport and keep asking for directions. Just before the waterfall a small restaurant serves *patacones* and drinks. Alternatively, you can hire horses to take you there. Another horse-riding trip is to **El Valle de Los Ríos**, a valley in the jungle with several crystalline rivers and beautiful waterfalls. The primary forest in this area is rich in wildlife; you might see, among other animals, sloths, howler monkeys, toucans, parrots, fishing eagles and several types of lizard and iguana. You should take a guide for this. The trip includes lunch at a *ranchería*. For more details, enquire at **Capurganá Tours** in town, by the jetty, or at the football pitch (*cancha de futbol*) in the village centre.

Another trip is to Sapzurro, a few kilometres north (see below). **Capurganá Tours** organizes day trips to the **San Blas Archipelago** in Panama, possibly some of the most beautiful islands in the Caribbean, and launches stop at the island of **Caledonia**.

There is excellent diving and snorkelling around Capurganá. You are likely to see nurse sharks, moray eels, spotted eagle rays, trumpetfish, jewfish, barracuda and hawksbill turtles, among other species, as well as large brain and elkhorn coral. Several of the hotels organize diving and the independent dive centre, **Dive and Green**, near the jetty, is recommended. ►► *See What to do, page 54.*

Sapzurro

Sapzurro is a quiet little village in the Darién and the last outpost before Panama and Central America. Set in a shallow, horseshoe-shaped bay dotted with coral reefs, little happens in this village of less than 1000 inhabitants. There are no roads, let alone cars; the houses are linked by intersecting pathways bursting with tropical flowers. It has a couple of excellent little hostels and some good restaurants serving up home-cooked seafood. The bay is excellent for snorkelling, with a couple of underwater caves to explore.

You can make a day trip to the small village of **La Miel** over the border in Panama by walking up the forested hill behind the village. This could qualify as the most relaxed border crossing in the world. The Colombian and Panamanian immigration officers share a hut and copy each other's notes. Be sure to take your passport; if only going to La Miel they won't stamp it but they will take your details. There are breathtaking views of Panama and back into Sapzurro at the border crossing on the brow of the hill.

La Miel has a gorgeous white-sand beach with beautiful, clear waters and a coral reef. The snorkelling is relatively good though a little low on fauna. There are a couple of shacks selling beer and food. Try the sea snails in coconut sauce. You can arrange for a launch to pick you up and take you back to Sapzurro or Capurganá.

Around Cartagena listings

For hotel and restaurant price codes and other relevant information, see pages 9-13.

🛏 Where to stay

Islas del Rosario *p44*
$$$$ Kokomo Islas del Rosario, Caño Ratón–Isla Grande, www.hotelkokomo.com. All-inclusive private beach resort, pool and restaurant, transport to and from the island.
$$$$ Isla del Pirata, book through Excursiones Roberto Lemaitre, T665 2952, www.hotelislapirata.com. Simple, comfortable *cabañas*, activities include diving, snorkelling, canoeing and petanque, good Caribbean restaurant. Prices include transport to the island, food and non-guided activities. Highly recommended.

Isla Grande
$$$$ San Pedro de Majagua, book at C del Torno, No 39-29, Cartagena, T650 4460,

www.hotelmajagua.com. Everything from a 'pillow menu' to Egyptian cotton bed sheets, this is a lovely, luxurious place for utter relaxation.
$$$ Ecohotel La Cocotera, Comunidad de Orika, www.ecohotellacocotera.com. Rooms with bath and solar power, also has camping and hammocks, restaurant, diving school.

Mompós *p45, map p46*
It is essential to book in advance for Semana Santa and other festival periods, when prices go up.
$$$ Bioma, C Real del Medio (Cra 2), No 18-59, T685 6733, www.bioma.co. Boutique style, cool and fresh, courtyard garden with running water, jacuzzi on roof terrace and a small pool. Rooms are large, mostly white, family rooms have 2 floors. There's a restaurant but reserve in advance.
$$$ Hostal Doña Manuela, C Real del Medio (Cra 2), No 17-41, T685 5621/5142,

hostalmompox@turiscolombia.com.
A converted colonial merchant's house,
an enormous, lovely building with a huge
tree in the 1st courtyard which is home to
many bats. Only a few rooms were open in
2012, quiet and peaceful, good restaurant,
pool open to the public for the day US$2.
Good service, knowledgeable managers.
Art gallery and jewellery shop. Check in
advance if it is open.

$$$-$$ La Casa Amarilla, Cra 1, No 13-59,
T685 6326, www.lacasaamarillamompos.
com. A block up from the Iglesia Santa
Bárbara near the riverfront, 3 standards of
room, master suites and suites, cheaper
'colonial' rooms, and a small dorm (US$9 pp),
beautifully decorated. All rooms open onto
a cloister-style colonial garden. English
owner Richard McColl is an excellent source
of information on Colombia. Laundry, book
exchange, use of kitchen, roof terrace,
bicycle hire, tours arranged to silver filigree
workshops and to wetlands for birdwatching
and swimming (US$10 pp). Recommended.

$$ Casa de España, C Real del Medio
(Cra 2), No 17A-52, T313-513 6946,
hotelcde@hotmail.com. White rooms,
some for families, pool to be built.

$ Casa Hotel Villa de Mompox, Cra 2,
No 14-108, 500 m east of Parque Bolívar,
T685 5208, casahotelvilladecmompox@
yahoo.com. Charming, family-run, decorated
with antique bric-a-brac. Also arranges
rooms for families during festivals.

$ La Casona, Cra 2, No 18-58, T685 5307,
eusedeal@yahoo.es. Fine colonial building
with delightful courtyards and plants.

$ San Andrés, C Real del Medio (Cra 2),
No 18-23, T685 5886, hotelsanandres24@
hotmail.com. Another fine, restored colonial
building, with nice sitting room and garden.
Rooms for 1-5 people, cheaper with fan, on
a corridor off the garden, spacious, use of
kitchen, meals extra. Same owner as Islandés
restaurant and tour company (river tours).

Tolú *p48*

$$ Alcira, Av La Playa, No 21-151, T288
5016, alcirahotel@yahoo.com. Modern, on
the promenade, with restaurant and parking.

$$ pp Estado Natural Ecolodge, 7 km from
San Bernardo del Viento, T320-573 4121,
www.estado-natural.com. Rustic cabins
on a beach, composting toilets and other
sustainable practices, meals not included,
cabins have kitchen, activities include
birdwatching, windsurfing, trips to Isla
Fuerte, riding and guided tours.

$$ Villa Babilla, C 20, No 3-40, Barrio el
Cangrejo, T312-677 1325, www.villababilla
hostel.com. Run by a Colombian/German
team. 3 blocks from the beach, well
organized, dorms and private rooms, good
restaurant, good information on diving and
island tours. Recommended travellers' hostel.

$$-$ Mar Adentro, Av La Playa 11-36, T286
0079, www.clubnauticomaradentro.com.
Belonging to the good tour agency of the
same name. Nice rooms, cheaper with fan.

$ El Turista, Av La Playa, No 11-20, T288 5145.
The cheapest option in town and good value
for money. Next to all the tour agencies.

Isla Múcura

$$$$ Punta Faro, Isla Múcura, Islas San
Bernardo, T318-216 5521, www.punta
faro.com. Low-key luxury resort with
45 rooms in a gorgeous setting by the sea,
inside Corales del Rosario National Park.
Price includes all meals (buffet-style) and
return boat transfer from Cartagena (boats
leave once a day in high season and
Mon and Fri only in low season). Massage
treatments, hammocks on the beach,
eco walks around the island and a good
sustainability policy. Highly recommended.

Coveñas

There are plenty of hotels in Coveñas,
many catering for family holidays.

$$$ Porto Alegre, Primera Ensenada, T313-
815 7889, www.hotelportoalegre.com.co.
Beachfront hotel, rooms for 2-5 people,
with a/c, microwave, pool, jacuzzi, breakfast

included, no restaurant but can arrange meals with nearby establishments, similarly tours.
$$ La Candelita, Primera Ensenada de Punta Piedra, T313-777 6399, www.la candelita.com. Simple cabins for 2 to 6 people, with a/c or fan, TV; principally a watersports centre, including kitesurfing lessons, kayaks, sailing, boat trips.

Arboletes p49
$$$-$$ El Mirador, C Principal, T820 0441, www.hotelelmiradordearboletes.com. Self-styled 'boutique' hotel with 14 rooms, some with bunk beds (**$** pp), includes breakfast, restaurant and bar, jacuzzi, internet and parking.
$ La Floresta, C Principal, T820 0034. This small hotel has simple rooms with private bathrooms and a/c. Ask for a street-facing room if you want a window.

Turbo p49
$$ Castilla de Oro, C 100, No 14-07, T827 2185. The best option in town, has a/c, safety box, minibar, a good restaurant and a swimming pool. Modern building with reliable water and electricity. Friendly staff.
$$ Simona del Mar, Km 13 Vía Turbo, T824 3729, www.simonadelmar.com. Turbo is not a safe place to walk around at night, so this is a better, safer option for sleeping. A few kilometres outside town, this hotel has a number of *cabañas* in a tranquil setting and near the beach. Good restaurant. The beach is nice enough, although like everywhere on this stretch of the coast, the sea is a muddy brown due to its proximity to the Gulf of Urabá. A taxi to and from Turbo is US$11. You can also ask *colectivos* to drop you there.

Capurganá p50
Accommodation and food are generally more expensive than in other parts of Colombia. Upmarket options include Tacarcuna Lodge (www.hotelesdecosta acosta.com/capurgana) and Bahía Lodge (www.bahia-lodge.com).

$$ Cabaña Darius, T314-622 5638, www.dariuscapurgana.es.tl. In the grounds of Playa de Capurganá, excellent value, simple, comfortable rooms in tropical gardens, fan, breakfast included.
$$ Marlin Hostal, Playa de los Pescadores, T824 3611, capurganamarlin@yahoo.es. The best mid-range option in town, good rooms, also bunks (**$**), good restaurant serving excellent fish.
$ Hostal Capurganá, C del Comercio, T316-482 3665, www.hostalcapurgana.net. Comfortable, pleasant patio, well situated. Recommended.
$ Luna Verde Hostel, T313-812 7172, www.capurgana-sanblas.com. With double rooms, dorms and hammocks, offers diving, snorkelling, treks and other activities, plus trips to San Blas and Panama.
$ Posada del Gecko, T314-525 6037, www.posadadelgecko.com. Small place, 5 rooms with bath and 3 cabins, gardens, popular café/bar that serves good Italian food.

Sapzurro p51
$ Paraíso Sapzurro, T824 4115/313-685 9862, www.paraiso-sapzurro-colombia.com. *Cabañas* on the beach at the southern end of the village, Chilean-run (ask for El Chileno), higher price includes halfboard. Also has space for camping (US$3 or US$4 with tent hire).
$ Zingara Cabañas, Camino La Miel, T313-673 3291. Almost the last building in Colombia, 2 lovely *cabañas* overlooking the bay. The owners have a herb and vegetable garden and sell home-made chutneys. This also doubles up as the village pharmacy.

❶ Restaurants

Mompós p45, map p46
$$$-$$ El Fuerte, Parque Santander, T685 6762/314-564 0566, www.elfuertemompox. com. In the art gallery of Walter Maria Gurth in a restored colonial building, displaying his wooden furniture, occasionally serves gourmet pizza. Contact in advance.

$ Comedor Costeño, on the riverfront between calles 18 and 19. Good local food, popular for lunch.

$ Islandés, on the riverfront between calles 18 and 19. In same vein as Comedor Costeño and almost next door, same owner as San Andrés (see Where to stay).

$ Plaza Santo Domingo, outside the church of that name. Every night stallholders sell freshly cooked food, also fresh juices. The best nights to go are Wed-Sun.

Capurganá *p50*
$$ Donde Josefina, Playa La Caleta, T316-779 7760. Josefina cooks exquisite seafood, served to you under a shady tree on the beach. Try the lobster cooked in garlic and coconut sauce.

○ Shopping

Mompós *p45, map p46*
Mompós is famous for its filigree gold and silver jewellery and its wicker rocking chairs. Several jewellers can be found on C del Medio (Cra 2). You can visit workshops.

Jewellery
Filimompox, Cra 2, No 20-132, tallersanta cruz@yahoo.com. Also for jewellery.
Joyería Sam, C 18A No 2B-31, T685 5829. Fine selection of beautifully worked gold and silver earrings, bracelets and brooches.
Santa Cruz, Cra 2, No 17-76. Another jewellery shop.

Rocking chairs
Muebles Momposinos, Cra 2, opposite Monumento del Sagrado Corazón, T685 5349.

○ What to do

Islas del Rosario *p44*
Diving
Cultura del Mar, Getsemaní C del Pozo, No 25-95, Cartagena, T664 9312. Offices in Cartagena, organizes snorkelling and diving, and various tours of the coral reefs and mangroves of the islands.

Excursiones Roberto Lemaitre, C 6 No 2-26, Edif Granada, local 2, Bocagrande, T665 5622 (owner of Club Isla del Pirata, www.hotelislapirata.com). They have the best boats and are near the top end of the price range but Yates Alcatraz is more economical; enquire at the quay.

Tolú *p48*
Tour operators
Club Náutico Mar Adentro, Av La Playa, No 11-36, T286 0079, www.clubnautico maradentro.com. A good agency offering tours to the islands, diving, has its own 35-room hotel, connections with Hotel Darimar and can organize lodging at other hotels and *cabañas* in the area.

Capurganá *p50*
Diving
Dive and Green, near the jetty, T682 8825, www.diveandgreen.com. Dive centre offering PADI and NAUI, lots of courses and snorkelling. Excursions to San Blas. English spoken. Also has rooms to let.

Tour operators
Capurganá Tours, C del Comercio, T316-382 3665, www.capurganatours.net. Organizes walking tours with knowledgeable guides to nearby beaches and into the jungle as well as horse riding, diving and birdwatching. Trips to San Blas islands in Panama arranged if sufficient people. Can assist in booking flights from Puerto Obaldía to Panama City. English spoken. Highly recommended.

○ Transport

Mompós *p45, map p46*
Air
The closest airport is **Corozal** (near Sincelejo), which has regular connections with **Medellín** and **Bogotá**. It's 1 hr by *colectivo* from Corozal airport to Magangué, or 15 mins from Corozal to Sincelejo, then take a *colectivo* to Magangué, as below.

Bus and ferry

There is no road between Magangué and Mompós. You have to take a fast *chalupa* (motorized canoe, 20 mins, life jacket provided), or the vehicle ferry (1 hr, food and drink on board) to/from La Bodega, then continue by road. Passengers can also take the vehicle ferry Magangué–La Bodega, free if you arrive as the ferry is leaving. In Magangué it leaves from Yati, about 2 km outside town. The 1st vehicle ferry leaves La Bodega at 0600.

From **Cartagena** (see page 24): direct bus with **Unitransco**, or **Brasilia**, at 0630, 8 hrs, US$23, bus returns at 0430 from outside Iglesia Santa Bárbara (same fare Barranquilla–Mompós, 8½ hrs). **Toto Express**, T310-707 0838, runs a door-to-door *colectivo* service between Mompós and **Cartagena**, 6-7 hrs, US$40. Or take a **Cootransabanas Express** *colectivo* Trans 54, No 94-06, Vía Estrella, from petrol station outside Cartagena bus terminal to Magangué, 0600-1700, 4 hrs, US$22, then *chalupa* to La Bodega, US$4, and finally *colectivo* to Mompós, 1¼ hrs, US$6. **Asotranstax** runs a door-to-door *colectivo* service between Mompós and **Santa Marta**, leaves Santa Marta 0300 and 1100, 6 hrs, US$40. To **Medellín**, *colectivo* to La Bodega, then *chalupa* to Magangué and finally bus with **Brasilia**, 12 hrs, US$57, or from Magangué take a *colectivo* to **Sincelejo**, US$9, 1½ hrs, then a **Brasilia** or **Rápido Ochoa** bus to Medellín, 8-10 hrs, US$57. For **Valledupar**–Mompós, see under Valledupar.

From **Bogotá**, **Copetran** and **Omega** have services to **El Banco** at 1700, 14 hrs, US$50, then take a 4WD to Mompós, US$16.50 (US$19.50 a/c), 1 hr. **Note** prices for public transport rise Dec-Jan and at Easter.

Tolú *p48*
Bus

Brasilia hourly to **Cartagena** between 0715 and 1730, US$20. 12 a day to **Medellín** with Brasilia and Rápido Ochoa, US$61, via Montería.

Turbo *p49*
Bus

From **Medellín**, buses every 1½ hrs to Turbo, 10-12 hrs, US$25-35. To **Montería**, 4-5 hrs, US$18. Fewer from **Cartagena**. Check safety carefully before travelling by road to/from Turbo.

Sea

Launches for **Capurganá** leave daily at 0700-0900, 3 hrs, US$30, T312-701 9839. Turbo's port is known as El Waffe. It's a spectacular journey that hugs the Caribbean shoreline of Darién. Rush for a seat at the back as the journey is bumpy and can be painful in seats at the front. **Note** Make sure that all your belongings, especially valuables, are in watertight bags and be prepared to get wet. There is a 10 kg limit on baggage, excess is US$0.30 per kg. From mid-Dec to end Feb the sea is very choppy and dangerous. We advise you not to make the journey at this time.

Capurganá *p50*
Air

1 flight daily to **Medellín** with Aerolínea de Antioquia (ADA, www.ada-aero.com), US$200 one way. Same company from Medellín to **Acandí**, about 3 a week, US$150 one way. Twin Otter biplanes with 16 passenger capacity. Be sure to book ahead. Baggage limit of 10 kg. Excess is US$2 per kg. Your baggage may have to follow on a later plane if seriously overweight.

Sea

See above for boats to/from **Turbo**. Boat Capurganá–**Acandí** US$10.50.

There are launches to **Puerto Obaldía** in Panama, US$15 (leaving at about 0700). From here it's possible to catch an **Air Panamá** flight to **Panama City** on Sun, Tue or Thu, cost US$85, www.flyairpanama.com. Essential to book in advance.

Sapzurro *p51*
You can walk to **Capurganá** in 4 hrs,
a beautiful hike along the coastline
through jungle rich in wildlife.

Sea
Launches to **Capurganá** cost US$7, 30 mins.
Launch to **Puerto Obaldía** 45 mins, US$15.
Launches leave from Puerto Obaldía or
La Miel to **Panama**.

⊙ Directory

Mompós *p45, map p46*
Banks There are ATMs on C 18 by the
junction with C del Medio.

Tolú *p48*
Banks There are several banks with ATMs
on the Parque Principal.

Capurganá *p50*
Immigration Ask Migración Colombia
in Cartagena, Medellín (C 19, No 80A-40
in Belén La Gloria section, T4-345 5500)
or Montería (C 28, No 2-27, T 4-781 0841,
cf.monteria@migracioncolombia.gov.co,
Mon-Fri 0800-1200, 1400-1700) whether
the immigration office in Capurganá is open.
If leaving for Panama you must get your
passport stamped before leaving Colombia.
Check with the Panamanian embassy
(www.empacol.org) or a consulate
about current entry requirements.

Barranquilla

Barranquilla, Colombia's fourth city, lies on the western bank of the Río Magdalena, about 18 km from its mouth. It's a seaport (though less busy than Cartagena or Santa Marta), as well as a river port, and a modern industrial city with a polluted but colourful central area near the river. Many people stay a night in Barranquilla because they can find better flight deals than to Cartagena or Santa Marta. It's worth a short stay as the city is growing as a cultural centre, safety has improved and there are several things to do and see. It's also a good place to buy handicrafts, which are the same as can be found elsewhere but cheaper.

First and foremost, however, Barranquilla is famed for its carnival, held 40 days before Easter (end of February/beginning of March). It's reputed to be second only to Rio de Janeiro in terms of size and far less commercialized. In 2003 UNESCO declared it a "masterpiece of the oral and intangible heritage of humanity". Pre-carnival parades and dances last through January until an edict that everyone must party is read out. Carnival itself lasts from Saturday, with the *Batalla de las Flores*, through the *Gran Parada* on Sunday, to the funeral of Joselito Carnaval on Tuesday. The same families have been participating for generations, keeping the traditions of the costumes and dances intact. Prepare for three days of intense revelry and dancing with very friendly and enthusiastic crowds, spectacular floats, processions, parades and beauty queens.

Arriving in Barranquilla → *Phone code: 5.*

Getting there and around
Ernesto Cortissoz Airport ① *www.aerocivil.gov.co*, is 10 km from the city. A city bus from the airport to town costs US$0.90 (more on Sunday). Only take buses marked 'centro'; you can catch them 200 m from the airport on the right. Taxis are booked at the central taxi kiosk; tell them your destination and you will be given a ticket with the price to pay the driver at end of ride. A taxi to the centre costs US$12.35 and takes about 30 minutes. On the ticket is a phone number for a 20% discount on return to the airport. There is an ATM outside the terminal entrance, a *casa de cambio* in the hall (closed after 1900), and a tourist information desk. The main **bus terminal** ① *Km 1.5 Prolongación Murillo, www.ttbaq.com.co*, is south of the city near the Circunvalación. City buses cost US$0.90, a little more on Sunday. The **Transmetro** is a dedicated bus service with two routes, *Troncal Murillo* and *Troncal Olaya Herrera*. It takes prepaid cards; single journey US$0.90 (US$0.95 on Sunday and holidays). Take the Transmetro to Terminal de Transporte for long-distance buses. Taxis for trips within town cost US$4 (eg from downtown to the northern suburbs). ▸▸ *See Transport, page 62.*

Tourist information
Secretaría de Cultura, Patrimonio y Turismo ① *C 34, No 43-31, p 4, T339 9450, www.barranquilla.gov.co/cultura*. The **Comité Mixto de Promoción de Atlántico** ① *Vía 40, No 36-135, La Aduana, T330 3866, www.visitbarranquilla.travel*, has a Facebook page which lists upcoming events. Tourist information is also available at the main hotels. The best place for information carnival is the official office **La Casa de Carnaval** ① *Cra 54, No 49B-39, T319 7616, www.carnavaldebarranquilla.org*.

🗓 Barranquilla centre

Where to stay 🛏
Barranquilla Plaza **1**
Cayenas **2**

Girasol **3**
San Francisco **4**

Transmetro buses ———

Places in Barranquilla

The city is surrounded by a continuous ring road called the 'Vía Cuarenta' from the north along the river to the centre; 'Avenida Boyacá' to the bridge (Puente Pumarejo), which crosses the Río Magdalena for Santa Marta; and 'Circunvalación' round the south and west of the city. The long bridge over the Río Magdalena gives fine views.

The new **Catedral Metropolitana** ① *Cra 45, No 53-120, opposite Plaza de la Paz*, has an impressive statue of Christ inside by the Colombian sculptor, Arenas Betancur. The church of **San Nicolás**, formerly the cathedral, stands on Plaza San Nicolás, the central square, and before it is a small statue of Columbus. The commercial and shopping districts are round Paseo Bolívar, the main boulevard, a few blocks north of the old cathedral, and in Avenida Murillo (Calle 45). A brand new cultural centre, **Parque Cultural del Caribe**, has opened at the Paseo Bolívar end of Avenida Olaya Herrera (Carrera 46). It contains the **Museo del Caribe** ① *C 36, No 46-66, T372 0581, www.culturacaribe.org, Mon-Fri 0800-1700, Sat-Sun 0900-1800, ticket office closes 1600 (1700 weekend), closed 1st Mon of month, US$6*, an excellent introduction to the region, in Spanish only, but guided tours in English are available. Visits start on the top floor, at the Sala García Márquez, which has audiovisual displays and a library. Work your way down through floors dedicated to nature, indigenous people and cultures, to a video musical presentation at the end. Outside is a large open

② Barranquilla – El Prado

→ **Barranquilla maps**
1 Barranquilla centre, page 58
2 Barranquilla –El Prado, page 59

400 metres
400 yards

N

Where to stay ▭	Restaurants 🍴	Bars & clubs 🍸
Bulevard 58 **3**	Arabe Gourmet **1**	Froggs Leggs **6**
El Prado **2**	Arabe internacional **2**	Henry's **7**
Majestic **4**	Firenze Pizza **3**	La Troca **9**
Meeting Point **1**	La Cueva **4**	
	La Parilla Libanesa **8**	Transmetro buses ———
	Los Helechos de Carlos **5**	

space for theatre and children's games, and the **Cocina del Museo** restaurant. Not far away is the restored customs house (1919) **Antiguo Edificio de la Aduana** ① *Vía 40 y C 36*, which has historical archives. The **Museo Romántico** ① *Cra 54, No 59-199, Mon-Fri 0900-1200, 1430-800, US$2.75*, covers the city's history with an interesting section on carnival.

There are good parks to the northwest of the centre, including **Parque Tomás Suri Salcedo** on Calle 72. Stretching back into the northwestern heights overlooking the city are the modern suburbs of **El Prado**, Altos del Prado, Golf and Ciudad Jardín, where you'll find the **El Prado Hotel**. There is a full range of services including commercial and shopping centres, and banks between Bulevar Norte and Avenida Olaya Herrera towards the Country Club.

Barranquilla also attracts visitors because the most important national and international football matches are held here in Colombia's largest stadium, **Estadio Metropolitano** ① *Av Murillo, south of the city*. The atmosphere is considered the best in the country. There are four other stadiums in the city, for sports such as football, basketball and baseball.

Around Barranquilla

Regular buses from Paseo Bolívar and the church at Calle 33/Carrera 41 go to the attractive bathing resort of **Puerto Colombia** ① *19 km, www.puertocolombia-atlantico.gov.co*, with its pier built around 1900. This was formerly the ocean port of Barranquilla, connected by a railway. The beach is clean and sandy, though the water is a bit muddy. The **Hotel Pradomar** ① *C 2, No 22-61, T309 6011, www.hotelpradomar.com*, has a good beach bar, **Climandario Sunset Lounge**, and restaurant. It also offers surfing lessons, as does surf school **Olas Puerto Colombia** ① *T313-817 0111, www.olascolombia.com*. February to May is the best time for taking classes; the biggest waves are November to January. Nearby are the beaches of **Salgar**, and north of Barranquilla is **Las Flores** (2 km from the mouth of the Río Magdalena at Bocas de Ceniza); both are good places for seafood.

South along the west bank of the Magdalena, 5 km from the city, is the old colonial town of **Soledad**. The cathedral and the old narrow streets around it are worth seeing. A further 25 km south is **Santo Tomás**, known for its Good Friday flagellants who symbolically whip themselves as an Easter penance. There are also street theatre presentations at this time. The small town of **Palmar de Varela** is a little further along the same road, which continues on to Calamar.

Vía Parque Isla de Salamanca ① *US$19.25 for non-nationals, US$7.20 for Colombians*, is a national park, across the Río Magdalena from the city, comprising the Magdalena Delta and the narrow area of beaches, mangroves and woods that separate the Ciénaga Grande de Santa Marta (see page 68) from the Caribbean. Its purpose is to restore the mangroves and other habitats lost when the highway to Santa Marta blocked off the channels that connect the fresh and salt water systems. There is lots of wildlife, but it is not yet geared up for tourism.

Barranquilla listings

For hotel and restaurant price codes and other relevant information, see pages 9-13.

🛏 Where to stay

Barranquilla *p57, maps p58 and p59*
Hotel prices rise significantly during carnival; it's essential to book well in

advance. Most people stay in the north zone, beyond the Catedral Metropolitano, C 50. There are a few hotels in the business zone, Cra 43-45, C 42-45.

$$$$-$$$ El Prado, Cra 54, No 70-10, T369 7777, www.hotelelpradosa.com.
A landmark in Barranquilla, this enormous hotel with 200 rooms has been around

since 1930 and still retains some of its old-fashioned service. Fantastic pool shaded by palm trees, various restaurants, tennis courts and a gym.

$$$$-$$$ Sonesta, C 106, No 50-11, T385 6060, www.sonesta.com. Overlooking the Caribbean, a 1st-class business hotel with fitness facilities and restaurant to match. There is a shopping centre and nightclub nearby.

$$$ Barranquilla Plaza, Cra 51B, No 79-246, T361 0333, www.hbp.com.co. A deluxe hotel popular with Colombian businessmen, it's worth visiting just for the 360° view of the city from its 26th-floor restaurant. It has all the other amenities you would expect of a hotel of this standard, including gym, spa, sauna and Wi-Fi.

$$$ Majestic, Cra 53, No 54-41, T349 1010, www.hotelmajesticbarranquilla.com. An oasis of calm in the city, with large, fresh rooms, it has a fine pool and a restaurant serving the usual fish and meat dishes and sandwiches.

$ Meeting Point, Cra 61, No 68-100, El Prado, T368 6461, ciampani@gmail.com, www.facebook.com/meetingpointhostel. barranquilla. Italian/Colombian-owned, the best choice for budget travellers. Mixed dorms or women only, US$13-16.50, cheaper with fan and shared bath, also has a private room, very helpful and congenial, eating places and cultural centres nearby. Warmly recommended.

Business district

$$ Girasol, C 44, No 44-103, T379 3191, www.elhotelgirasol.com. Safe, central with a helpful manager, it has a restaurant and a functions room.

$$ San Francisco, C 43, No 43-128, T351 5532, www.sfcol.com/barranquilla.html. Bright rooms, courtyard full of songbirds, a good, safe bet, with restaurant.

$ Cayenas, C 43, No 44-136, T370 6912, hotelcaycnas@yahoo.com. A simpler option, welcoming, rooms are cheaper with fan.

🍽 Restaurants

Barranquilla *p57, maps p58 and p59*
In Barranquilla you'll find places to suit all tastes and budgets. Many upmarket restaurants can be found along Carreras 52-54 from C 70 to 93. There are numerous good Arab restaurants, especially Lebanese, in Barranquilla due to waves of Arab immigration in the 20th century, also Chinese restaurants and pizzerias.

$$$-$$ Arabe Gourmet, Cra 49C, No 76-181. More formal and expensive than other Arabic restaurants. There are others in the same chain.

$$$-$$ La Cueva Cra 43, No 59-03, T379 0342, www.fundacionlacueva.org. Formerly a high-class brothel and a favourite haunt of Gabriel García Márquez and his literati friends during the 1950s. Its bohemian charm may have gone, but it's a Museo Centro Cultural, with a bar/restaurant and recommended for a visit. Good typical food, live music and other events.

$$$-$$ La Parrilla Libanesa, Cra 61, No 68-02, T360 6664, near **Meeting Point**. Well-regarded Lebanese place, colourful, indoor and terrace seating.

$$ Arabe Internacional, C 93, No 47-73, T378 2803. Good Arab cuisine in an informal setting.

$$ Firenze Pizza, C 68, No 62-12, El Prado, T344 1067, near **Meeting Point**. Eat in or take-away.

$$-$ Los Helechos de Carlos, Cra 52, No 70-70, T356 7493. Offers *comida antioqueña* in a good atmosphere.

🍸 Bars and clubs

Barranquilla *p57, maps p58 and p59*
Froggs Leggs, C 93, No 43-122, T357 4661, http://www.froggleggs.tv. Popular bar, good atmosphere.

Henry's Café, C 80, No 53-18, CC Washington, T345 6431. Popular US-style bar and restaurant. Open daily from 1600.

La Troca, Cra 44, No 72-263. Popular for salsa, not far from the old stadium.
Salsa 8, Cra 8, No 33A-79. In an excellent area which is popular for nightlife. Take a taxi there and back.

🎭 Entertainment

Barranquilla *p57, maps p58 and p59*
Teatro Amira de la Rosa, Cra 54, No 52-258, T369 2410, www.banrepcultural.org/amira-de-la-rosa. This modern theatre offers a full range of stage presentations, concerts, ballets, art exhibitions, etc, throughout the year.

🎉 Festivals

Barranquilla *p57, maps p58 and p59*
Jan/Mar Carnival, tickets for the spectator stands are sold in major restaurants and bars. For more information, contact **La Casa de Carnaval**, www.carnavaldebarranquilla.org. Carnival is a long-standing tradition in Barranquilla, lasting for the 4 days before Ash Wed, comparable to the carnivals of Rio de Janeiro and Trinidad. Events begin in Jan. As always on such occasions, take special care of your valuables.

🛍 Shopping

Barranquilla *p57, maps p58 and p59*
There is a good-value handicrafts market near the old stadium, which is at Cra 46 y C 74 (at the end of Transmetro).

🚌 Transport

Barranquilla *p57, maps p58 and p59*
Air
See Arriving in Barranquilla, page 58, for airport information. The bus to the airport (marked Malambo) leaves from Cra 44 up C 32 to Cra 38, then up C 30 to airport.

Daily flights to **Bogotá**, **Cali**, **Cúcuta**, **Medellín**, **Bucaramanga**, **Montería** and **Valledupar**. International flights to **Miami** and **Panama City**.

Airline offices Avianca, C 53, No 46-38, T349 1257, and Cra 46, No 85-152, T378 6579, at airport T334 8396. Copa, C 72, No 54-49, loc 1 y 2. **LAN**, C 75 No 52-56 local 3. **EasyFly**, T385 0676. Viva Colombia, T319 7989.

Bus
To **Santa Marta** with Brasilia, US$7, 2 hrs. To **Valledupar**, 5-6 hrs, US$15.50. To **Bogotá**, 24 hrs, frequent, US$66 direct. To **Maicao**, US$27, 6 hrs (with Brasilia, frequent). To **Cartagena**, 2½-3 hrs, US$7-8, several companies. Brasilia Van Tours (Cra 35, No 44-63, T371 5226, as well as the bus terminal), and Berlinastur (Cra 43, No 71-43, T318-354 5454, Cra 46, No 95-27 and other offices), have minibus services to Cartagena and Santa Marta (US$8.25).

📖 Directory

Barranquilla *p57, maps p58 and p59*
Banks Many ATMs. *Casa de cambio* El Cairo, C 76, No 48-30, T360 6433. TCs, euros, dollars, Mon-Fri and Sat 0900-1200.
Embassies and consulates For your country's embassy or consulates in Colombia, see http://embassy.goabroad.com. Venezuela, Edif Concasa, Cra 52, No 69-96, p 3, T368 2207, http://barranquilla.consulado.gob.ve, open 0800-1500, visa issued same day, but you must be there by 0915 with all documents and US$30 cash; onward ticket may be requested.
Security Migración Colombia: Cra 42, No 54-77, T351 3401; Tourist police, Cra 43, No 47-53, T351 0415, T340 9903.

Santa Marta

Santa Marta, the capital of Magdalena Department, is the third Caribbean port, 96 km east of Barranquilla. It was the first town created in Colombia by the conquistadors, but it does not have the same concentration of colonial beauty as Cartagena. What it lacks in architecture it makes up for in character and activity, and the Samarios are some of the most welcoming and gregarious people you will find anywhere in Colombia. The area around Santa Marta has much to offer, including a number of beaches. Head west to the family resort of Rodadero, or north to the former fishing village of Taganga. Backpackers love Taganga's lazy charm; it's a convenient stopping point en route to Tayrona and a good place to organize treks to Ciudad Perdida in the Sierra Nevada de Santa Marta. Southeast is Ciénaga de Santa Marta, 4000 sq km of wetlands with all types of waterbirds. From Santa Marta you can also reach Aracataca, birthplace of Colombia's most famous writer, Gabriel García Márquez, and generally accepted as the inspiration for the village of Macondo which features in several of his books, including *One Hundred Years of Solitude*.

When leaving Santa Marta, most travellers will make a beeline for Tayrona National Park and its wild coastline of golden sands, secluded coves and tropical jungle. But there are other options. If the heat of the coast becomes too much, the rural village of Minca, in the foothills of the Sierra Nevada, will provide welcome respite.

Arriving in Santa Marta → *Phone code: 5.*

Getting there
The **Simón Bolívar Airport** is 20 km south of the city. A bus to town costs US$1 and a taxi to Santa Marta is US$10-15, less to Rodadero. If you arrive by bus, beware of taxi drivers who take you to a hotel of their choice, not yours. The **bus terminal** is southeast of the city, towards Rodadero, and a minibus to the centre of Santa Marta costs US$0.70; taxi to the centre US$3, or US$6 to Rodadero.

Orientation
Santa Marta lies at the mouth of the Río Manzanares, one of the many rivers that drain the Sierra Nevada de Santa Marta, on a deep bay with high shelving cliffs at each end. The city's fine promenade offers good views of the bay and is lined with restaurants, accommodation and nightlife, though none of a very high quality. At the southern end, where the main traffic turns inland on Calle 22, is a striking sculpture dedicated to the indigenous heritage of the region, La Herencia Tairona. The main commercial area and banks are mainly on Carrera 5 and Calle 15.

Getting around
Local bus services from Santa Marta to Rodadero cost US$1 (this is a flat fee all the way to the airport), and a taxi is US$4.50-5.50. Many of the buses coming from Barranquilla and Cartagena stop at Rodadero on their way to Santa Marta.

Tourist information
The **tourist office** ① *Plaza de la Catedral, C 16, No 4-15, T438 2587*, has helpful staff but not much information. The **national parks office** ① *C 17, No 4-06, Plaza de la Catedral, www.parquesnacionales.gov.co*, has an office for each of the four local parks.

Climate
This area is relatively humid but the on-shore winds moderate the temperature much of the time. February and March are pleasant months to visit.

Security
The north end of town near the port and the section beyond the old railway station are dangerous and travellers are advised not to go there alone, as it's rife with drugs and prostitution is common. South of Rodadero Beach has also been reported unsafe.

Background

This part of the South American coastline was visited in the early years of the 16th century by the new Spanish settlers from Venezuela. At this time, many indigenous groups were living on and near the coast, and were trading with each other and with communities further inland. The dominant group were the Tayrona.

Santa Marta was founded in 1525 by Rodrigo de Bastidas, who chose it for its sheltered harbour and its proximity to the Río Magdelena and therefore its access to the hinterland. Also, the *indígenas* represented a potential labour force and he had not failed to notice the presence of gold in their ornaments.

Within a few years, the Spanish settlement was consolidated and permanent buildings appeared (see the Casa de la Aduana, below). Things did not go well, however. The *indígenas* did not 'collaborate' and there was continual friction amongst the Spaniards, all of whom were expecting instant riches. Bastidas' successor, Rodrigo Alvarez Palomino, attempted to subdue the *indígenas* by force, with great loss of life and little success. The *indígenas* that survived took to the hills and their successors, the Kogi, are still there today.

By the middle of the 16th century, a new threat had appeared. Encouraged and often financed by Spain's enemies (England, France and Holland), pirates realized that rich pickings were to be had, not only from shipping, but also by attacking coastal settlements. The first raid took place around 1544, captained by the French pirate Robert Waal with three ships and 1000 men. He was followed by many of the famous sea-dogs – the brothers Côte, Drake and Hawkins – who all ransacked the city in spite of the forts built on a small island at the entrance to the bay and on the mainland. Before the end of the century more than 20 attacks were recorded and the pillage continued until as late as 1779, the townsfolk living in constant fear. Cartagena, meanwhile, became the main base for the conquistadors and much was invested in its defences. Santa Marta was never fortified in the same way and declined in importance. Over the years caches of treasure have been unearthed in old walls and floors – testimonies to the men and women of those troubled times who did not survive to claim them.

Two important names connect Santa Marta with the history of Colombia. Gonzalo Jiménez de Quesada began the expedition here that led him up the Río Magdalena and into the highlands to found Santa Fe de Bogotá in 1538; and it was here that Simón Bolívar, his dream of Gran Colombia shattered, came to die. Almost penniless, he was given hospitality at the *quinta* of San Pedro Alejandrino, see below. He died there on 17 December 1830, at the age of 47.

Places in Santa Marta → *For listings, see pages 75-81.*

In the city centre, well-preserved colonial buildings and early churches still remain and more are currently being restored. There has been much investment in new business, such as bars and restaurants on Carrera 3, the hub of nightlife in the centre. Much of Carrera 3 and Calle 19 are pedestrianized and Carrera 5 has many kerbside stalls. The centre of Santa Marta is the pleasant and leafy Plaza Bolívar, which leads down to the seafront. It is complete with statues of Bolívar and Santander, and a bandstand. On the north side is the **Casa de la Aduana/Museo de Oro** ① *C 14, No 2-07*, which became the Custom House when Santa Marta was declared a free port in 1776. Previously it belonged to the Church and was used as the residence of the Chief Justice of the Inquisition. The house dates from 1531 and was probably the first built of brick and stone in Colombia. An upstairs garret, added in 1730, offers an excellent view of the city and the bay. Simón Bolívar stayed here briefly in December 1830 and he lay in state on the second floor from 17 December to the 20 December before being moved to the cathedral. The Custom House now displays an excellent archaeological collection, with four rooms of exhibits mainly dedicated to the indigenous Tayrona. Especially interesting is the model of Ciudad Perdida, the most important of the Tayrona cities. At the time of writing Casa de la Aduana was closed for conservation work. Usually contained within the building, the **Museo de Oro (Gold Museum)** ① *Mon-Fri 0830-1800, Sat 0900-1300, free*, has been temporarily moved to the library of Banco de la Repúblic next door. There are a number of pre-Columbian gold artefacts held in the vault.

The original building on the site of the **cathedral** ① *Cra 4, C 16/17, open for Mass daily at 0600 and 1800 (more frequently on Sun), and you may find it open at 1000*, was completed a few years after the founding of the city and was probably the first church of Colombia as proclaimed by the inscription on the west front. The present building is mainly 17th century with many additions and modifications, hence the mixture of styles. There are interesting

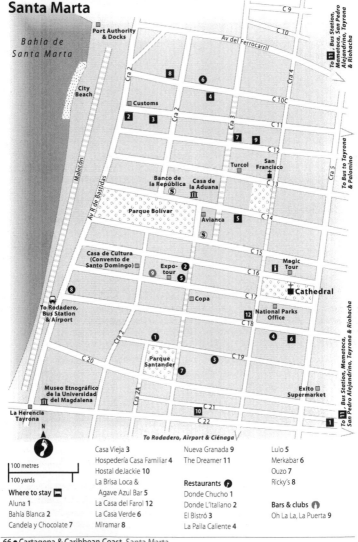

Santa Marta

Bahía de Santa Marta

Port Authority & Docks
City Beach
Customs
Av del Ferrocarril
Cra 1
Cra 2
Cra 3
Cra 4
Cra 5
C 9
C 10
C 10C
C 11
C 12
C 13
C 14
C 15
C 16
C 17
C 18
C 19
C 20
C 21
C 22
Cra 2A

Malecón
Av R de Bastidas

Banco de la República ⑤
Casa de la Aduana 🏛
Parque Bolívar
Avianca ⑤
Casa de Cultura (Convento de Santo Domingo) 🏛
Expo-tour
Copa
Turcol
San Francisco
Magic Tour
✝ Cathedral
National Parks Office
Parque Santander
Museo Etnográfico de la Universidad del Magdalena 🏛
La Herencia Tayrona
Exito Supermarket

To Rodadero, Bus Station & Airport
To Rodadero, Airport & Ciénaga

To Bus Station, Mamatoca, San Pedro Alejandrino, Tayrona & Riohacha
To Bus to Tayrona & Palomino
To Bus Station, Mamatoca, San Pedro Alejandrino, Tayrona & Riohacha

N
100 metres
100 yards

Where to stay 🛏
Aluna 1
Bahía Blanca 2
Candela y Chocolate 7
Casa Vieja 3
Hospedería Casa Familiar 4
Hostal deJackie 10
La Brisa Loca & Agave Azul Bar 5
La Casa del Farol 12
La Casa Verde 6
Miramar 8
Nueva Granada 9
The Dreamer 11

Restaurants 🍴
Donde Chucho 1
Donde L'Italiano 2
El Bistró 3
La Paila Caliente 4
Lulo 5
Merkabar 6
Ouzo 7
Ricky's 8

Bars & clubs 🍸
Oh La La, La Puerta 9

shrines along the aisles, a fine barrel roof and chandeliers, and a grey Italian marble altar decorated with red and brown, the whole giving a light, airy and dignified impression. Notable is the monument to Rodrigo de Bastidas, founder of the city, to the left of the main entrance and the inscription by the altar steps commemorating the period when Bolívar's remains rested here from his death in 1830 to 1842 when they were transferred to the Pantheon in Caracas. The **Convento de Santo Domingo** ① *Cra 2, No 16-44, open to the public Mon-Fri 0900-1200, 1500-1900*, now serves as a cultural centre and houses a library. It has a tree-filled patio. **Museo Etnográfico de la Universidad del Magdalena** ① *Cra 1, C 22, p 2, T431 7513, Mon-Sat 0800-1900, US$3*, has good displays tracing the history of Santa Marta, its port and the Tayrona culture.

Quinta de San Pedro Alejandrino ① *daily 0930-1700 (high season 0900-1730), US$6.60, discounts for students and children; take a bus or colectivo from the waterfront, Cra 1 C, in Santa Marta, to Mamatoca and ask for the Quinta, US$0.50*, an early 17th-century villa, is 5 km southeast of the city and dedicated to sugar cane production. This is where Simón Bolívar lived out his last days and the simple room in which he died, with a few of his personal belongings, can be visited. Other paintings and memorabilia of the period are on display in the villa, and a contemporary art gallery featuring works by artists from Venezuela to Bolivia (the countries associated with Bolívar's life), and an exhibition hall have been built on the property. The estate and gardens, with some ancient cedars, *samanes*, dignified formal statues and monuments, can be visited. It is an impressive memorial to the man most revered by Colombians.

Around Santa Marta → *For listings, see pages 75-81.*

All along this stretch of coast are rocky headlands, sandy bays and coves, surrounded by hills, green meadows and shady trees. The largest bay is that of Santa Marta, with Punta Betín, a promontory, protecting the harbour to the north and a headland to the south on top of which are the ruins of an early defensive fort, Castillo San Fernando. The rugged Isla El Morro lies 3 km off Santa Marta and is topped by a lighthouse. The proximity of the port and the city means the beach is not recommended for bathing. There is a marine ecosystem research science centre, run by Colombian and German universities, near the end of Punta Betín. ►► *For further information on nearby beaches, see Tayrona National Park, page 69.*

Rodadero and around

Rodadero Beach, 4 km southwest of Santa Marta, is one of the best along this coast. It is part of the municipality of **Gaira**, a small town 2 km away, alongside the main road, on the Río Gaira which flows into the Caribbean at the southern end of Rodadero Beach. The main part of the beach has high-rise hotels of all standards, but it is attractive, tree lined, relatively clean and pleasant for bathing. Behind the promenade are the restaurants, cheaper accommodation and services. Nearby are a number of holiday flats and other holiday centres operated by public and social entities. Rodadero is a popular destination for family holidays. There is a waterpark popular with kids and families at the southern end of the main beach (0900-1700, US$6). **Fondo de Promoción Turística** ① *C 10, No 3-10, T422 7548*, can provide local information and advice on hotels.

Launches leave Rodadero Beach for the 10-minute trip to the **Aquarium** ① *Cra 1 y C 8, T422 7222, www.acuariorodadero.com, open from 0900, US$15.50, under 5s US$1, including boat transport*, north along the coast at Inca Inca Bay, where you'll find sharks, dolphins, seals and many colourful fish of the Caribbean. The aquarium is linked to a small museum housing relics from Spanish galleons sunk by pirates, and a collection of coral and seashells. The boats leave from the beach at the end of Calle 12 every hour from 0800 and the last boat back leaves at 1630. Evening and day-long boat tours are offered (US$16-30), as well as photos and swimming with dolphins (US$77). From the aquarium, you can walk (10 minutes) to the **Playa Blanca** and swim in less crowded conditions. There is also food available at this beach.

Ciénaga de Santa Marta

The paved coast road to Santa Marta from Barranquilla passes salt pans and skirts the Ciénaga de Santa Marta. There is a wildlife sanctuary, recognized by UNESCO and RAMSAR, which is not open to visitors, but many water birds, plants and animals can be seen on and around the large lake. Cutting off the egress from the lake to the sea to build the coast road killed large areas of mangrove and caused an ecological disaster, but a National Environment Programme is working to reopen the channels and restore the area. There are two villages built on stilts in the lake, **Nueva Venecia** and **Buenavista**. Ask at the **Santuario de Flora y Fauna Ciénaga Grande de Santa Marta** desk in the national parks office in Santa Marta (see page 64) about guides and boatmen who take visitors to the lake from the community of Tasajera. On the east shore of the lagoon is **Ciénaga**, which is famous for *cumbia* music.

Taganga and around

Close to Santa Marta is the former fishing village (most people now make a living from tourism) and beach of Taganga. From Santa Marta it takes 15-20 minutes by minibus

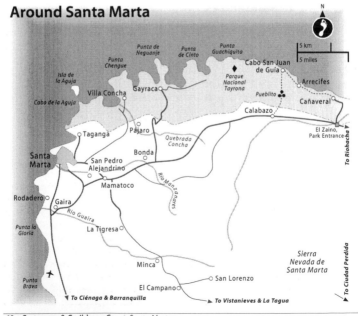

Around Santa Marta

(US$0.50) or taxi (US$4). Set in a tranquil semi-circular bay surrounded by scorched hills dotted with cacti, Taganga attracts its fair share of backpackers and has become quite a party resort. It is laid back and welcoming, but beaches east of Tayrona National Park are becoming more favoured as 'in' places on the backpacker circuit. The swimming is good, especially on **Playa Grande**, 25 minutes' walk round the coast, but do not leave your belongings unattended. Taganga is even more popular at weekends. Boat trips along the coast for fishing, and to the many bays and beaches are run by hotels and by a syndicate of boatmen along the beach.

Half an hour north of Taganga is **Isla de la Aguja**, a good fishing zone. **Playa Granate**, is nearer and has excellent places to snorkel and dive around the coral reefs, although lately the reefs have been showing signs of bleaching.

Parque Nacional Tayrona → *For listings, see pages 75-81.*

The beaches of Tayrona National Park are what you would expect of a tropical paradise: thick jungle teeming with wildlife spills over onto golden sand beaches, some with pounding surf, and there are small, secluded bays, excellent for swimming and sunbathing. There is something of the prehistoric about Tayrona. Squint your eyes and with a little imagination the flocks of pelicans that glide overhead become pterodactyls, the bright-tailed lizards that scurry underfoot as you walk through the forest paths reminders of their extinct cousins and the enormous boulders that stand guard over the beaches look like they have been there since the beginning of time. However, time and tourism have caught up with Tayrona and it is becoming increasingly popular. Prices have rocketed and there is now a steady stream of visitors, especially during the national holidays of Semana Santa, July-August and December-January.

The park is named after the Tayrona (also spelt Tairona) culture, one of the most important of pre-colonial Colombia. It extends from north of Taganga for some 85 km of rugged coastline much of it fringed with coral reefs. You will see monkeys, iguanas and maybe snakes.

Arriving in Parque Nacional Tayrona
Getting there The park has four entrances: **Bahía Concha**, the closest to Santa Marta (entry US$3.85); **Palangana** for Neguanje and Playa Cristal; **Calabazo** for Pueblito and Cabo San Juan de Guía; **El Zaino**, at the east end of the park, 35 km from Santa Marta, for Cañaveral and Arrecifes. El Zaino is the most commonly used point of entry and is where you sign in and buy a ticket. From the gate *colectivos* make the 4-km journey to the visitor centre at Cañaveral (see below), US1.10, or it is possible to walk (approximately one hour).

Park information The park is open 0800-1700; tickets cost US$19.25 for foreigners regardless of age, US$7.20 Colombians (US$3.85 children), parking extra. Sometimes the park closes temporarily for a variety of reasons, but never for long. It is best to arrive early. The address of national parks office in Santa Marta is given on page 64. Information can also be found on the **Colombian Tourist Board – Proexport**'s website, www.colombia.travel, and the national parks' website, www.parquesnacionales.gov.co.

Hiking boots may be useful and there are sometimes bloodsucking insects to contend with. There are food and drink stands in the park, or you can take your own food and water. If you are staying overnight in one of the campsites or hammock places, remember to take all supplies with you (but only the essential valuables as robbery has been a problem) as there is only a small store in the park at Cañaveral. You can hire horses to carry you and your luggage from Cañaveral to Arrecifes, US$9; US$13 to La Piscina; and US$17.50 to Cabo San Juan (one way). Littering was a big problem in the past, but there are now camouflaged litter bins along all the main trails and around the campsites. In the wet, the paths are very slippery. Guides, who charge US$20 or more per person, are available, but you will not need one for the main trail from Cañaveral to Arrecifes and beyond. It is advisable to inform park guards when walking anywhere in the park other than the main trail.

Around the park

Many of the bays are accessible by road, including the beautiful beach at **Villa Concha**, 5 km from the eastern edge of Santa Marta at Bastidas. Surrounded by tree-covered hills and with several restaurants nearby, the bay is popular with locals at the weekend and makes a good day trip during the week.

The beaches of **Bahía Concha**, **Neguanje** and **Playa Cristal** (a 10-minute boat ride from Neguanje) can be reached from Santa Marta by tours (eg from hostels), or in the case of Neguanje, by *colectivos* from the market, which leave at 0700 and return at 1600.

The normal entry to the park is the turning off the main road at El Zaino, 35 km from Santa Marta and at the eastern end of the park. From there, a road leads 4 km to the administrative and visitor centre at **Cañaveral**, where there is a gift shop, a car park, a museum (closed) and the trail of Nueve Piedras, to a mirador (about 30 minutes there and back). A few metres from the car park is a juice bar, campsite, the road to the **Ecohabs** (see Where to stay) and horse hire at the start of the trail to Arrecifes. It is a one hour walk through the forest from Cañaveral to **Arrecifes**. The trail is mostly level, apart from a couple of short, steep sections. At Arrecifes, beyond the cabins, campsites and eating places, is a long beach backed by mangroves. On no account be tempted to swim here as the tides and surf are treacherous. Every year, people drown because they do not heed the warnings. Walk on from Arrecifes to **La Piscina**, 40 minutes further. You pass a little beach, **La Arenilla**, two-thirds of the way along, with a *cevichería* and juice stall. La Piscina also has a couple of places selling drinks, one of which also sells food. The beach is narrow, but the swimming after the walk is divine and there is excellent snorkelling. From La Piscina you can walk on to **Cabo San Juan de Guía**, 45 minutes, which also has excellent bathing, places to eat and a popular campsite/hammock place. From Cabo San Juan you can return the way you came, take the boat to Taganga, or walk 1½ hours on a clear path up to the archaeological site of **Pueblito**. A guided tour around the site is free, every Saturday, or as arranged with a park guard. Other Tayrona relics abound. At Pueblito there are indigenous people; do not photograph them. From Pueblito you can continue for a pleasant two-hour walk up to Calabazo on the Santa Marta–Riohacha road. It is possible to do a circuit Santa Marta–Cañaveral–Arrecifes–Pueblito–Calabazo–Santa Marta in one day, but you will need to leave by 0700 at the latest. It is easier (more downhill) to do the circuit in reverse; ask to be dropped at Calabazo. Tours can be arranged at several hotels and agencies in Santa Marta.

East of Tayrona

Beyond El Zaino on the Santa Marta–Riohacha road is **Los Angeles**, with access to fine empty beaches, excellent for surfing. Tours can be arranged at the **Cabañas Los Angeles**, www.cabanasantamartalosangeles.com, the owner is Nohemi Ramos who also offers tours). Ten minutes west of Los Angeles is the mouth of the Río Piedras, the border of Tayrona National Park, where you can bathe and enjoy sights to rival those in the park. At **Quebrada Valencia** ① *US$1.20*, are several natural swimming pools amid waterfalls, with

The Lost City

From the first day we set out on the trail toward the mysterious Colombian Lost City, until day six when the remarkable adventure into the heart of the sierra came to an end, I was blown away by the crystal-clear rivers that cascaded down from the upper reaches of the mountains and treated us to amazing natural swimming pools, beautiful waterfalls and a much welcomed respite after hours of hiking amidst the endless jungle landscape. There are 18 or so river crossings en route to the Lost City, river pools to swim in each day and 1200 stone steps to climb at the very end of the third day that take you above the gorgeous river valleys to the high ridges blanketed in green. While the site alone is impressive, and its mysterious history and late discovery only add to its splendour, the surrounding mountain peaks dominate the endless landscape. What else lies undiscovered and hidden among such wild, rugged and beautiful terrain?

Despite the unsettling events in 2003, when eight foreigners were kidnapped along the Lost City trail, the region is currently considered safe and is heavily patrolled by the Colombian Army. The site is guarded day and night by about 40 friendly soldiers who pass their two month assignment on site by asking visitors for cigarettes in exchange for odd looking nuts that they have picked up off the jungle floor. They will also obligingly pose for photos, which they seem to enjoy more than anything else.

There is more than one option when it comes to choosing a route, some a little more difficult and with longer days, but the rewards will outweigh the fatigue. Starting and finishing the hike in different places will give you the chance to see more of the remote landscape and travel to less visited parts of this unique mountain range. For more information on trekking, see page 72.

Craig Weigand

good views. From the marked roadside entrance, it is a pleasant 20-minute walk along a clear path, or horse ride, to the waterfalls. It can get overcrowded during high season. Drinks and snacks are available along the way. The paved coastal road continues from Tayrona and crosses into Guajira Department at increasingly popular **Palomino**, 80 km from Santa Marta, which has a fine beach, a river running into the sea and fine views of the Sierra Nevada, including snow-capped Pico Bolívar. There are hotels, hostels and *cabañas*, with more under construction.

Ciudad Perdida → *For listings, see pages 75-81.*

Ciudad Perdida (Lost City) is the third of the triumvirate of 'must-sees' on Colombia's Caribbean coast (the other two being Cartagena and Tayrona). The six-day trek is right up there with the Inca Trail in Peru and Roraima in Venezuela, as one of the classic South American adventures and is a truly memorable experience.

The site

Ciudad Perdida was called Teyuna by the Tayrona, meaning 'mother nature'. The city covers 400 ha and was built around AD 700. It stands at 1100 m on the steep slopes of Cerro Corea, which lies in the northern part of the Sierra Nevada de Santa Marta. It was the political and trading centre of the Tayrona. The site covers 400 ha and consists of a complex system of buildings, paved footpaths and flights of steps which link a series of terraces and platforms, on which were built cult centres, residences and warehouses. The Tayrona built sophisticated irrigation systems and walls to prevent erosion. The living quarters housed some 1400-3000 people. By around 1600, the Tayrona were almost wiped out by the conquistadors and the few who survived were forced to flee. For the next four centuries, the city disappeared under the forest growth. In 1973, tomb looters searching for gold known to exist in burial urns and graves, rediscovered the city by chance. By 1975, the city was officially re-found, attracting local and international anthropologists and archaeologists who started to excavate, leading to the first tourist groups in 1984. Today the area is a protected indigenous reserve, where three main indigenous groups, the Koguis, Arhuacos and Arsarios (Wiwa), continue to live.

Trekking

The 20-km trek to the Lost City is, at times, gruelling and challenging. It is not a leisurely walk, but is well worth the effort for a rewarding and memorable experience. The trek is perhaps as spectacular as the archaeological site itself. Depending on the length of tour, it starts and ends at Machete Pelao or El Mamey. Along with lush tropical humid and dry forests, abundant flora and fauna, there are crystal-clear rivers, waterfalls and natural swimming pools. There are some 1200 steep slippery steps to climb to the summit of the city; the nearest campsite to the city is below these steps. Watch out for snakes. Along the way, you will pass friendly Kogui villages. Don't forget that Ciudad Perdida is in a national park: it is strictly forbidden to damage trees and collect flowers or insects. Only four agencies are licensed to take tours to Ciudad Perdida (see What to do, page 79). The price covers park permits (entry is US$10 for non-Colombians). For archaeological information, contact **ICANH** ① *C 12, No 2-41, Bogotá, T444 0544, www.icanh.gov.co.*

Sierra Nevada de Santa Marta → For listings, see pages 75-81.

① *Entry US$11. For the latest information check with national parks offices in Santa Marta and Bogotá and the Fundación Pro Sierra Nevada C 17, No 3-83, Santa Marta, T431 0551, www.prosierra.org.*
The Sierra Nevada, covering a triangular area of 16,000 sq km, rises abruptly from the Caribbean to 5800-m snow-capped peaks in about 45 km, a gradient comparable with the south face of the Himalaya, and unequalled along the world's coasts. Pico Colón is the highest point in the country. Here can be found the most spectacular scenery and most interesting of Colombia's indigenous communities. The area has been a drugs-growing, processing and transporting region. For this reason, plus the presence of guerrilla and paramilitary groups, some local *indígenas* have been reluctant to welcome visitors, but the situation is improving and limited activities are now possible, such as the trek to Ciudad Perdida. From Valledupar, it is also possible to enter the sierra, with permission from community leaders.

Minca

① *Catch a bus from C 11 with Cra 11 in Santa Marta (30 mins, US$2). A taxi will cost US$15.*
If the heat of the coast becomes too much then a stay up in Minca is a refreshing alternative. Some 20 km from Santa Marta in the foothills of the Sierra Nevada, this small village, surrounded by coffee *fincas* and begonia plantations, is a popular excursion and offers several cheap and truly charming places to stay. Horse riding, birdwatching and tours further into the Sierra Nevada can be arranged from here.

About 45 minutes' walk beyond the village is **El Pozo Azul**, a local swimming spot under a waterfall, popular at weekends but almost always empty during the week, well worth a visit. El Pozo Azul was a sacred indigenous site where purification rituals were performed and on occasion it is still used by the Kogi of the Sierra Nevada.

San Lorenzo

Beyond Minca, the partly paved road rises steeply to San Lorenzo which is surrounded by a forest of palm trees. On the way to San Lorenzo is **La Victoria**, a large coffee *finca* which offers tours to demonstrate the coffee-making process. It is possible to stay in *cabañas* run by the park authorities near San Lorenzo.

Near San Lorenzo is the **El Dorado Bird Reserve**, the perfect place to see the majority of the 19 bird species endemic to the Sierra Nevada de Santa Marta. It is managed by **ProAves** ① *Cra 20, No 36-61, Bogotá, T1-340 3229, www.proaves.org*, a Colombian NGO dedicated to the conservation of biodiversity, especially birds at risk of extinction. There is a lodge at the reserve and all visits must be arranged through ProAves and its associated tour operator, **Eco Tours** ① *www.ecotours.org*. They run seven-day tours which include Minca and Guajira, or more specialist itineraries at set times.

Inland from Santa Marta → *For listings, see pages 75-81.*

Aracataca

Aracataca, 60 km south of Ciénaga and 7 km before Fundación, is the birthplace of Gabriel García Márquez. It was fictionalized as Macondo in some of his novels, notably in *One Hundred Years of Solitude*. His home is now a **Casa Museo** ① *take Cra 5 away from plaza at corner with Panadería Delipán, the museum is next to La Hojarasca café, open 0800-1700, with a break for lunch*. Different rooms have objects and quotations from his work in Spanish and English to provide an overview of his family life. You can also visit the **Casa del Telegrafista**, which houses a few dusty items (ask Tim at **The Gypsy Residence**, see Where to stay, page 77, to open it if no one is there, leave a donation). **Finca Macondo** (named after a type of tree) is possibly a source of inspiration for García Márquez' choice of the name. It is 30 minutes from town. You can visit it in an afternoon; take a mototaxi, US$16.50 with wait. Other sites related to the stories are the river, where you can swim, and the railway station, through which coal trains pass.

Valledupar

South of Aracataca and Fundación is the important road junction of Bosconia (80 km). The main road continues to Bucaramanga while a road east goes towards Maicao and the Venezuelan border and a road west heads to the Río Magdalena (a side road at La Gloria on this road goes towards Mompós – see Transport, below). The easterly route goes 89 km to **Valledupar**, capital of César Department, on the plain between the Sierra Nevada de Santa Marta and the Sierra de Perijá. Continuing on this road takes you **Cuestecitas**, where you can turn north to Riohacha, or carry on to Maicao.

Valledupar is the home of *vallenato* music and culture. On the main Plaza Alfonso López Pumarejo is the cultural centre **Fundación Festival de la Leyenda Vallenata: Compai Chipuco** ① *C 16, No 6-05, T580 8710, tiendacompaichipuco@festivalvallenato.com*, a good place for information. It sells handicrafts, books and music and has a bar, restaurant and photographic exhibition of *La Cacica*, Consuelo Araujonoguera, one of the founders of **El Festival de la Leyenda Vallenata** (www.festivalvallenato.com), who was murdered by

Gabriel García Márquez

More than any other Colombian, Gabriel García Márquez, or Gabo as he is affectionately known, has shaped the outside world's understanding of Colombian culture. His books champion the genre of magical realism where the real and the fantastical blur so naturally that it is difficult to discern where one ends and the other begins.

But is this what life in Colombia is really like? Schoolteachers-turned-dictators who fashion a town's children into an oppressive army, a woman so beautiful she causes the death of anyone who courts her and a child born with his eyes open because he has been weeping in his mother's womb seem improbable, especially to sceptical Western sensibilities. Yet many of the places, events and characters are based on real life. Macondo, a place which features in so many of his stories, is modelled on his town of birth, Aracataca. Cartagena is easily recognizable as the unnamed port that is the setting for *Love in the Time of Cholera*, while Fermina Daza and Florentino Ariza's love affair is based on his own parents' marriage. Events in *Chronicle of a Death Foretold* and *The Story of a Shipwrecked Sailor* were inspired by real life stories lifted from newspaper articles.

"Owing to his hands-on experience in journalism, García Márquez is, of all the great living authors, the one who is closest to everyday reality", wrote the American literary critic Gene H Bell-Villada, and who can challenge Gabo's interpretation of the truth when Colombia has produced real life characters such as Pablo Escobar? Where else in the world are there villages that host donkey beauty contests or elect a mayor who dresses up as a superhero? Sometimes Colombian reality is stranger than Gabo's fiction.

FARC in 2001. The festival, which takes place 26-30 April, draws thousands of visitors. Also of interest are **Escuela Vallenato Rafael Escalona** ⓘ *C 15, No 6-95*, with photos of famous artists and personalities, and **Sayco** ⓘ *Cra 5 No 13C – 40*, a good private collection. There are other cultural events throughout September.

Also on the Plaza Alfonso López Pumarejo is the **Iglesia Nuestra Señora de la Concepción** and the fine balconied colonial façade of the **Casa del Maestre Pavejeau**, in front of which is the dramatic statue of La Revolución en Marcha, by Rodrigo Arenas Betancourt. Around the city are many other statues, some to symbols and instruments of *vallenato*. The Río Guatapurí runs cold and clear from the Sierra Nevada past the city. The **Balneario Hurtado** is a popular bathing spot, especially at weekends, with food, drink and music (the water is muddy after heavy rain). It is by the bridge just past the Parque de la Leyenda, the headquarters of the Vallenato Festival; a statue of a mermaid, La Sirena, overlooks the bathers from the trees. From the centre take Carrera 9, the main commercial avenue, or, if cycling, the quieter Carrera 4. Across the bridge is **Ecoparque Los Besotes** (9 km), a dry forest wildlife reserve, good for birdwatching. A full-day tour from the city is to **La Mina** (20 km), a natural swimming pool by magnificent rocks, also popular at weekends. Another good excursion is to the Arhuaco community of **Nabusímake** ⓘ *from Cra 7A, where it splits from Cra 7 (beyond 5 Esquinas), take a bus 1 hr to Pueblo Bello at 0600, then a jeep to Nabusímake, 1 a day, 2-2 ½ hrs, US$7.75*, one of the most important centres of indigenous culture in the Sierra Nevada de Santa Marta. You have to stay the night as the jeep comes straight back. In Valledupar the **Casa Indígena** (Avenida Simon Bolivar, just past the accordion statue at end of Carrera 9), is where the Indians from the sierra gather. Go here if you need permission to visit remote places.

Santa Marta listings

For hotel and restaurant price codes and other relevant information, see pages 9-13.

⊙ Where to stay

Santa Marta *p63, map p66*
Do not stay at the north end of town near the port and beyond the old railway station, nor south of Rodadero Beach. In Rodadero itself there are resort hotels and holiday apartments. It's essential to book ahead during high season, particularly weekends, when some hotels increase their prices by 50%.
$$$$ La Casa del Farol, C 18, No 3-115, T423 1572, http://lacasadelfarol.com. A luxury boutique hotel with 6 rooms, all with its own style, roof terrace with pool, price includes breakfast, all modern conveniences, laundry service, beauty salon with massages.
$$$ La Casa Verde, C 18, No 4-70, T431 4122, www.casaverdesantamarta.com. Only 5 rooms, standard or suite, in attractive 'boutique' style, safe, with Wi-Fi, cable TV, small jacuzzi pool and juice bar. A *'desayuno típico'* (breakfast) is available.
$$$ Nueva Granada, C 12, No 3-17, T421 1337, www.hotelnuevagranada.com. This charming old building in the historic quarter has rooms round a pleasant courtyard, quiet, cheaper with fan, **$** in shared rooms, safety-deposit in rooms, small pool with jacuzzi, bike for guests to borrow, includes breakfast and welcome drink. Reductions in low season. Recommended.
$$ Aluna, C 21, No 5-72, T432 4916, www.alunahotel.com. Irish-run, pleasant, large hostel in a converted 1920s villa, central and convenient. It has private rooms and dorms (US$11-16.50 pp), with roof terrace. Breakfast is extra. There's a café and a good noticeboard. Recommended. Under the same ownership is **Finca Entre Ríos**, 1 hr from Santa Marta, a working farm with rooms to stay, full board **$$** pp.

$$ Bahía Blanca, Cra 1, No 11-13, T421 4439, www.hotelbahiablanca.com. Rooms around a pleasant courtyard, helpful staff, rooms cost less with fan than with a/c, cheaper in low season. Good.
$$ Casa Vieja, C 12, No 1C-58, T431 1606, www.hotelcasavieja.com. **$$$** in high season. Has a Spanish feel about it with white tiling and simple, clean rooms and a/c. Cheaper with fan, welcoming, it has a good popular restaurant.
$ Candela y Chocolate, C 12, No 3-01, T421 0977, www.candelaychocolate.com. Small B&B with dorm rooms only, for 5, 6 or 8 beds (US$12 pp, the smallest room has shared bath), all with fan, breakfast included in price, lockers, communal kitchen.
$ pp The Dreamer Hostel, Cra 51, No 26D-161 Diagonal, Los Trupillos, Mamatoco, T433 3264, or T300-251 6534, www.thedreamer hostel.com. Travellers' hostel in a residential district 15 mins from the centre, 5 mins by taxi from the bus station. All rooms are set around a sunny garden and pool, dorms for 4-10 people and private rooms with and without bath (**$$**), fan or a/c, bar, good Italian restaurant, tour information and activities, good atmosphere. All services close at hand, including a huge shopping mall, San Pedro Alejandrino and the bus stop for Tayrona. Recommended.
$ Hospedería Casa Familiar, C 10C, No 2-14, T421 1697, www.hospederia casafamiliar.freeservers.com. Run by an extremely helpful family, rooms with fan, roof terrace where you can cook your own food, bicycles for hire. Has its own dive shop and organizes trips to Tayrona and Ciudad Perdida. Recommended.
$ Hostal de Jackie, C 21, No 3-40, T420 6944, www.elhostaldejackie.com. Backpacker place with dorms for 4-12 people, US$12-17 pp, also a double dorm and private rooms with and without bath (**$$**). It has a kitchen for guests' use, serves breakfast, small pool.

$ La Brisa Loca, C 14, No 3-58, T431 6121, www.labrisaloca.com. Dorms from US$11 pp, US$26 with a/c, private rooms **$$**. US-owned, lively hostel, shared bath, meals extra, bar, swimming pool and billiard room.

$ Miramar, 2 blocks from Malecón, C 10C, No 1C-59, T423 3276, elmiramar_santa marta@yahoo.com. Very knowledgeable and helpful staff at this backpacker favourite. Can be crowded, simple dorms and some nicer more expensive private rooms (US$16.50), motorbike parking, cheap restaurant. Often full. Reservations via the internet (www.hosteltrail. com/hotelmiramar/) and are held until 1500 on the day of arrival. Tours to the Ciudad Perdida, Tayrona, Guajira and local sites are available at the in-house tour operator. Airline tickets also sold here.

Taganga *p68*

$$$ Bahía Taganga, C 8, No 1B-35, T421 0653, www.bahiataganga.com. Unmissable sign on the cliff face. Up on a hill at the north end of the bay it has commanding views over the village and is tastefully decorated with clean rooms. Breakfast is served on a lovely terrace, hospitable, a/c, more expensive in the new building.

$$$ La Ballena Azul, Cra 1, No 18-01, T421 9009, www.hotelballenaazul.com. Attractive hotel with French riviera touch, decorated in cool blues and whites, rooms open onto a central atrium with hanging bougainvillea and a palm tree. Comfortable, spacious rooms with sea views, also runs boat tours to secluded beaches, horses for hire. Nice restaurant on the beach, terrace bar.

$$ Casa Blanca, Cra 1, No 18-161, T421 9232, at the southern end of the beach, www.casa blancahosteltaganga.com. Characterful, each room has its own balcony with hammock, US$19 in dorm. The roof terrace is a fine place to pass the evening drinking beer with fellow guests, also has a tour desk.

$$ Techos Azules, Sector Dunkarinca, Cabaña 1-100, T421 9141, www.techos azules.com. Off the road leading into town,

cabañas with good views over the bay, private rooms and dorm US$14 pp (low season prices), free coffee, laundry service.

$$-$ Bayview, Cra 4, No 17B-57, T4221 9560, www.hosteltrail.com/bayview. With a technicolour façade, pleasant rooms, cheaper dorms (US$11 pp), kitchen, BBQ area, lounges with DVD player.

$$-$ Hostal Moramar, Cra 4, No-17B-83, T421 9202, www.hostalmoramar.com. 2 blocks uphill from beach opposite football pitch. Simple, quiet, dorm bed US$9.50, bright, airy, patio area, Wi-Fi, breakfast and laundry extra, attentive owners, welcoming.

$$-$ La Casa de Felipe, Cra 5A, No 19-13, 500 m from beach behind football field, T421 9101, www.lacasadefelipe.com. Cosy traveller place run by knowledgeable French team of Jean-Phillipe and Sandra Gibelin. Good kitchen facilities, excellent restaurant, hospitable, relaxing hammock and spacious garden area with sea views, studio apartments (**$$$-$$**), dorms (US$9-14) and rooms. Good information on trips to Tayrona (maps provided), English spoken. Highly recommended.

$ pp Divanga B&B, C 12, No 4-07, T421 9092, also **Casa Divanga**, C 11, No 3-05, T421 9217, www.divanga.com. French-owned hostel, doubles with private bath or 3-person dorm, includes great breakfast, comfortable, 5-mins' walk from beach, nice views, attentive service, lovely atmosphere, good pool, HI affiliated. Recommended.

$ Pelikan Hostal, Cra 2, No 17-04, T421 9057, www.hosteltrail.com/hostalpelikan. Rooms with fan for 2-7 people, restaurant.

Parque Nacional Tayrona *p69*

Comfortable upmarket cabins with thatched roofs (*ecohabs*) for 1-4 people cost from US$114 pp (half board, 4 people sharing, US$151 full board) at Cañaveral; cabins for 1-5 people at Arrecifes cost from US$78 pp (half board, US$121 full board; other packages available), bookable through

Aviatur (Av 19, No 4-62, Bogotá, T1-607 1500, www.concesionesparquesnaturales. com). They offer privacy as well as great views over the sea and jungle; both have decent restaurants. Both have campsites US$7 pp in 5-person tent; hammocks US$14. Take insect repellant and beware of falling coconuts and omnivorous donkeys.

Also at **Arrecifes** are various places to stay with double tents with mattress, US$22, hammocks, US$6.55 (US$8.20 with breakfast), US$4.50 to camp with own tent, toilets, meals. These include **Bukaru**, T310-691 3626; **El Paraíso**, T317-676 1614; **Los Bermúdez**, guide Luis Eduardo Muñoz, speaks English, viajesvara@hotmail.com, T310-741 4672, 300-499 0943, also run tours, eg to Sierra Nevada and Guajira; and **Yuluca** (there is also an ecohostel called **Yuluka** about 1 km from El Zaino entrance on the main road, www.eco-hostal-yuluka.com). At **Cabo de San Juan de Guía** there is a small restaurant and hammocks for hire (US$13 in high season, US$10 in low season); there are 2 *cabañas* on the rock that divides the 2 bays (US$50 high season, US$43 low); pitching your own tent costs US$7, tent hire for 2 people US$19.

East of Tayrona: Palomino
$$ Finca Escondida, Palomino, T315-627 5773, www.chillandsurfcolombia.com. Double rooms, dorms at US$13.50 pp, also camping and hammock space, direct access to the beach, which has good surf (surfing lessons and board rental available) and beach sports, bar-restaurant, prices rise in high season.
$ pp The Dreamer on the Beach, Playa Donaire, Palomino, T300-609 7229, www.onthebeach.thedreamerhostel.com. Brand new hostel from **The Dreamer** in Santa Marta, dorms and private suites (**$$$**), gardens, pool, restaurant, mini-market and access to activities.

Minca *p72*
$$$ Minca, on the hill to the right as you enter Minca, T421 9958/317-437 3078, www. hotelminca.com. Converted convent with views of the valley below, formerly called La Casona, fully remodelled, with breakfast, bath, fan, hot water, restaurant and bar, various activities including birdwatching.
$$ Sans Souci, Minca, T421 9968, sanssouciminca@yahoo.com. Rambling house in beautiful garden, German-owned, rooms in the house or separate apartments, swimming pool, kitchen, discount in exchange for gardening. Stunning views.
$$ Sierra's Sound, C Principal, Minca, T421 9993, www.sierrasound.es.tl. Italian-owned, overlooking a rocky river, hot water, home-made pasta, tours into the Sierra Nevada. There are many more places to stay in town.

Aracataca *p73*
$$-$ The Gypsy Residence, Cra 6, No 6-24, T321-251 7420, www.thegypsy residence.com. Run by Dutchman Tim Buendía, the best source of information on Aracataca. A great place to meet travellers and locals, Tim offers interesting tours of the town and surroundings. Just behind the Casa Museo, a/c, nice patio, it has a suite, a double room with shared bath and a 4-bed dorm. Recommended.

Valledupar *p73*
$$$ Sonesta, Diag 10, No 6N-15, T574 8686, www.sonesta.com. Business-class hotel, next to CC Guatapurí Plaza, it has all the usual amenities including a pool and restaurant.
$$$-$$ Vajamar, Cra 7, No 16A-30, T573 2010, www.hotelvajamar.com. This smart city centre hotel, whose rooms are cheaper at weekends, has a pool and an expensive restaurant.
$$ Hostal Provincia, C 16A, No 5-25, T580 0558, www.provinciavalledupar.com. Private rooms and dorms for 6, US$12.50 pp, which are cheaper with fan. A very good choice, with a nice atmosphere, free use of

bicycles, lots of information, helpful staff. Warmly recommended.
$$ La Casa de Siempre, Cra 7, No 15-53, T584 5254, hotellacasadesiempre@hotmail. com. In a colonial building in the centre, rooms contain lots of beds, no breakfast.

☺ Restaurants

Santa Marta *p63, map p66*
$$$-$$ El Bistró, C 19, No 3-68, T421 8080. Daily 1100-2300, happy hour 1700-1900. Meat dishes, pastas, salads, burgers, sandwiches and set lunches, neither a big place nor an extensive menu, wine list, Argentine influence throughout.
$$ Donde Chucho, C 19, No 2-07. A little expensive but well situated in the corner of Parque Santander. Serves mostly seafood.
$$ Donde L'Italiano, Cra 3, No 16-26. Mon-Sat 1130-1430, 1800-2230. Tasty Italian fare at reasonable prices, generous portions.
$$ La Paila Caliente, C 18, No 4-60. Delightful restaurant with good Colombian/ Caribbean food, à la carte at night, excellent value lunch, US$3.85.
$$ Ouzo, Cra 3, No 19-29. Mediterranean, Italian/Greek, seating on the street, popular restaurant and bar.
$$ Ricky's, Cra 1a, No 17-05. Beachside restaurant serving international food, including Chinese. Reasonably priced.
$$-$ Lulo, Cra 3, No 16-34, www.lulocafe bar.com. Café and bar serving *arepas*, wraps, paninis, fresh juices, coffee and cocktails.
$ Merkabar, C 10C, No 2-11. Opens early for breakfast. Pastas, great pancakes, good juices and seafood. Family-run, good value and provides tourist information. Recommended.

Taganga *p68*
Fresh fish is available along the beach and good pancakes can be found at the crêperie at the Hotel La Ballena Azul.
$$ Bitácora, Cra 1, No17-13. Seafood, pastas, burgers, steaks and salads, has a good reputation.

$ Yiu Nu Sagu, C 12, No 1-08.
Beachside pizzeria, large helpings.

Aracataca *p73*
$ Gabo, Cra 4. Serves good breakfast, lunch and, sometimes, dinner.
$ La Hojarasca, next to the Casa Museo. Juices, snacks and drinks, clean and pleasant.

Valledupar *p73*
There are some cafés on the Plaza Alfonso López, but all types of restaurant on Cra 9 from C 15 down, heading towards Plaza del Acordeón.
Café de Las Madres, Plaza de las Madres, Cra 9, No 15-19. A nice shady place, with a limited selection: coffee, beer, ices.

☺ Bars and clubs

Santa Marta *p63, map p66*
Santa Marta is a party town; new clubs, discos and bars open every week. In the evening wander along Cra 3 and C 17 and 18 either side of it to see what's going on.
Agave Azul, C 14, No 3-58. In the same building as La Brisa Loca, Mexican happy hour 1700-2000.
Oh La La, La Puerta, C 17, No 2-29. Excellent bar and atmosphere in a colonial house. Recommended.

Taganga *p68*
El Garaje, C 8, No, 2-127, T421 9003. Plays hip hop and other forms of electronic music. Starts late, finishes late.
Mojito Net, C 14, No 1B-61. Open 0800-0200, happy hour 1400-2100. Live music, open mic sessions, wine, cocktails, food and internet.

☺ Festivals

Santa Marta *p63, map p66*
Jul Festival Patronal de Santa Marta. Celebrates the founding of the city with parades and musical performances.
Jul Fiestas del Mar. Aquatic events and a beauty contest.

Aracataca *p73*
Sep Festival de Teatro Gitanos en **Macondo**, usually in the first week of the month, festival of theatre, mime, puppetry, with shows and educational events.

Valledupar *p73*
Apr Festival de la Leyenda Vallenata. See page 13 for details.

🛍 Shopping

Santa Marta *p63, map p66*
Craft shops
The **market** is at C 11/Cra 11, just off Av del Ferrocarril and has stalls with excellent selections of hammocks. There are several good handicraft shops on Parque Bolívar. **Artesanías La 15**, C15 with Cra 9, T310 730 9606, good selection of typical handicrafts; **Artesanías Sisa**, Cra 4, No 16-42 on the Plaza Catedral, T421 4510, local handicrafts including clothes, bags, hammocks and sombreros.

Valledupar *p73*
Centro Artesanal Calle Grande, C 16, block 7. Lots of stalls selling distinctive hats (you can pay anything between US$13 and US$1500), bags, jewellery, hammocks and some musical instruments.
Opposite is **Artesanías El Cacique**, C 16, No 7-23. See also above for **Fundación Festival de la Leyenda Vallenata: Compai Chipuco** on the plaza. **La Casa de la Música**, Cra 9, No 18-85. Record/CD shop.

🎯 What to do

Santa Marta *p63, map p66*
For guided trips to Quinta San Pedro Alejandrino and other local points of interest, ask at your hotel, travel agencies or the tourist office. Similarly, if you wish to visit the Marine Centre at Punta Betín you will need a boat or a permit to pass through the port area, so ask for guidance. For trips

to Ciudad Perdida and the Sierra Nevada, see under the relevant destination below.

Tour operators
New Frontiers Adventures, C 27, No 1C-74, close to Playa Los Cocos, T318-736 1565/317-648 6786, www.colombia. newfrontiersadventures.com. Trekking, birdwatching, diving and other adventures and ecotours, with English-speaking guides to Ciudad Perdida.
Turcol, C 13, No 3-13, CC San Francisco Plaza loc 115, T421 2256, www.buritaca 2000.com. Arranges trips to Ciudad Perdida, Tayrona, Pueblito, Guajira and provides a guide service.

Taganga *p68*
Adventure tours
Elemento, C 18. No 3-31, T421 0870, www.elementooutdoor.com. Mountain biking, hiking and other tours in the Sierra Nevada, Minca and Tayrona.

Diving shops
There are various dive shops in Taganga.
Oceano Scuba, Cra 2, No 17-46, T421 9004, www.oceanoscuba.com.co. PADI, NAUI, TDI and other courses, 2, 3 and 4 days.
Poseidon Dive Center, C 18, No 1-69, T421 9224, www.poseidondivecenter.com. PADI courses at all levels and the only place on the Colombian Caribbean coast to offer an instructor course. German owner, several European languages spoken. Own pool for beginners, also has rooms to rent (**$** pp), Wi-Fi.

Ciudad Perdida *p71*
Trips of 4-5 days are organized by 4 authorized agencies in Santa Marta: Turcol (see above), **Magic Tour** (C 16, No 4-41, Santa Marta, T421 5820, and C 14, No 1b-50, T421 9429, Taganga, www.magictourtaganga.com), **Expotour** (C 17, No 2-59, T421 9577, info@expotur-eco.com) and **Etnotur Wiwa** (C18, No 4-28, T423 5741). Other tour operators and hotels in Santa Marta or Taganga can

make arrangements. The cost is US$330 pp. Under no circumstances should you deal with unauthorized guides, check with the tourist office if in doubt.

All tours include transport to the start of the trail and back, sleeping in hammocks with mosquito nets, food, insurance, guides and entrance fees. The companies list the clothes and equipment you should take, such as sleeping bag, insect repellent, water bottle, etc. Accommodation is in organized camping or cabin sites. Tours run all year; be prepared for heavy rain. Leave no rubbish behind and encourage the guides to ensure no one else does. Going on your own is not allowed.

Minca *p72*
Semilla Tours, Minca, T313-872 2434, www. semillatours.com. Community tourism company offering tours in the region and elsewhere in Colombia. Also volunteering opportunities. Has its own guesthouse, **Finca La Semilla**, www.fincalasemilla.blogspot.co.uk.

⊖ Transport

Santa Marta *p63, map p66*
Air
There are daily flights to **Bogotá**, **Bucaramanga**, **Cali** and **Medellín**; connections to other cities. During the tourist season, get to the airport early and book well ahead (the same goes for bus reservations).

Airline offices Avianca, Cra 2A No 14-17, Edif de los Bancos, Local 105, T421 4958, T432 0106 at airport. **Copa**, CC Rex, Cra 3, No 17-27, local 2. **EasyFly**, T435 1777. **LAN**, C 23, No 6 – 18, local 2.

Bus
To **Bogotá**, 7 daily, 16 hrs, US$61, Brasilia or Berlinas del Fonce. Berlinas and Brasilia to **Bucaramanga** about 9 hrs, US$50, frequent departures 0700-2200. Buses to **Barranquilla**, 7 daily, 2 hrs, US$7; Berlinastur minibus, Cra 3, No 8-69, Rodadero, and terminal, T318-743 4343, US$8.25. To

Cartagena, 5 hrs, US$18, Brasilia. To **Riohacha**, 3 hrs, US$11. Frequent buses to **Maicao**, 4-5 hrs, US$14 a/c, cheaper non a/c.

Aracataca *p73*
Bus
Santa Marta–Aracataca, US$6.60 with Berlinas; to **Barranquilla**, US$8.25, goes via Ciénaga (US$6.60). To **Valledupar**, 3 hrs 45 mins, US$7 with **Cootracosta**. There may be a long stop in Fundación, but you don't have to change bus. To go to **Bucaramanga** (US$26) or **Bogotá** (US$36), you have to catch a bus coming from Santa Marta at the toll station (*peaje*) outside town 1½ hrs after the bus has left Santa Marta. Be at the toll 30 mins early. For information on all buses go to the **Berlinas** bus office.

Valledupar *p73*
Air
The airport is 3 km southeast of the town, close to the bus station, taxi, US$4.50. Flights from **Barranquilla** with EasyFly (T589 4010), 30 mins, and **Bogotá** with Avianca (T01-8000-953434) and LAN (Av Hurtado Diag 10N-6N, 15, CC Guatapuri, p 1, Plazoleta Juan Valdez), 1½ hrs.

Bus
The bus terminal is near the airport, taxi, US$4.50. To **Aracataca**, US$7, **Santa Marta**, 4 hrs, US$12, **Barranquilla**, 5-6 hrs, US$20, **Cartagena**, US$22, To **Mompós**, *puerta a puerta* with Lalo Castro, T312-673 5226, US$28.50; if he isn't going, **Veloz** or **Cootracegua** bus at 0400, 0800, or minibus from outside bus terminal to Santa Ana on the Río Magdalena, US$40, take a ferry across then a motorbike taxi to Mompós, US$5-8.

⊕ Directory

Santa Marta *p63, map p66*
Banks Banks with ATMs in Plaza Bolívar and Plaza San Francisco. *Casas de cambio* on C 13 entre Cras 5 y 6, and C14 entre Cras 4 y 5. **Exito** supermarket, in the block

bounded by C 19 y 20, Cra 5 y 6, has an ATM and a *cambio* which opens 1000-1300, 1400-1900, Sat 1000-1400. **Immigration** Migración Colombia, Cra 8, No 27-15, T421 7794. Mon-Fri, 0800-1200, 1400-1700.

Taganga *p68*
Banks ATM, all major credit cards, next to police station ½ block up from **Poseidon Dive Center**.

Valledupar *p73*
Banks ATMs in the **Exito** supermarket, Cras 6 y 7, C 16 y 17.

East to Venezuela

Along the coast from Santa Marta the lush vegetation of the foothills of the Sierra Nevada gives way to flat expanses of scorched earth where only a scrub-like tree known as trupillo (*Prosopis juliflora*) and the cactus survive. The change in landscape marks the beginning of the Guajira Peninsula, home to the Wayúu. It is also the northernmost tip of South America and it certainly feels like the end of the world; an arid and unforgiving terrain which nonetheless offers a home to vast flocks of flamingos and other birds and a chance to mingle with one of Colombia's best-preserved indigenous cultures. Riohacha may be a departmental capital but it feels more like a sleepy fishing village, though it livens up considerably at the weekend and on public holidays. Musichi and Manaure with their flocks of flamingos and salt works will be of interest to nature lovers and Cabo de la Vela with its turquoise waters that lap against a desert landscape is a sight to behold. If you have the time and energy, Parque Natural Nacional Macuira, an oasis of tropical green sprouting out of the semi desert, and Punta Gallinas, the northernmost point of the continent, will cap off a trip into this strange and sometimes ethereal land. The difficulties in transport only add to the sense of adventure this peninsula presents.

Riohacha → *For listings, see pages 87-90.*

Riohacha, 160 km east of Santa Marta, is capital of La Guajira Department. Formerly a port, today it has the ambience of a provincial fishing town. The city was founded in 1545 by Nicolás Federmann. One of Riohacha's resources of those days was oyster beds, and the pearls were valuable enough to tempt Drake to sack it. Pearling almost ceased during the 18th century and the town was all but abandoned. José Prudencio Padilla, who was born here, was in command of the Republican fleet that defeated the Spaniards in the Battle of Lago Maracaibo in 1823. He is buried in the cathedral, and there is a statue in the central park which bears his name. *Riohacha y Los Indios Guajiros*, by Henri Candelier, a Frenchman's account of a journey to the area 100 years ago, has very interesting depictions of the life of the Wayúu.

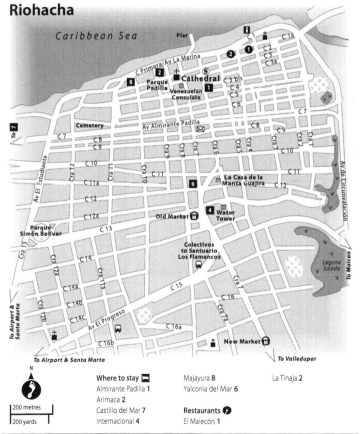

Riohacha

Where to stay 🛏
Almirante Padilla 1
Arimaca 2
Castillo del Mar 7
Internacional 4
Majayura 8
Yalconia del Mar 6

Restaurants 🍴
El Malecón 1
La Tinaja 2

200 metres
200 yards

Música tropical

No country in South America has a greater variety of musical genres than Colombia, and nowhere is music more abundant than in the fertile breeding grounds of the North Coast. The diversity of musical expression comes from a mixture of African, indigenous and European influences.

On the coast, *música tropical* is an umbrella term used to encompass the many hybrids that have arisen over the years. Most popular among these is *vallenato*, a form of music which originated with farmers around Valledupar and which primarily uses the accordion, *guacharaca* (a tube, made from the trunk of a small palm tree, with ridges carved into it, which when scraped with a fork produces a beat) and the *caja vallenata* (a cylindrical drum brought over by African slaves) as its instruments.

Vallenato is the current favourite but it has its roots in a more ancient genre,

cumbia. *Cumbia* began as a courtship dance practised among the slave population – it is believed to derive from Guinean *cumbe* – and later mixed with European and indigenous instruments, such as the guitar, the accordion and the *gaita*, a type of flute used by the *indígenas* of the Sierra Nevada de Santa Marta. *Cumbia* is celebrated for bringing together Colombia's three main ethnic groups and it was used as an expression of resistance during the campaign for Independence from the Spanish. *Cumbia* has many other derivatives, such as *porro*, *gaita*, *fandango* and *bullerengue*.

The newest genre to emerge is *champeta*. This is the most African of the genres, it takes its influence from *soukous* and *compas*, and is characterized by very sensual dancing. It gained popularity among the black population of Cartagena and San Basilio de Palenque in the 1980s.

Arriving in Riohacha
Getting there The José Prudencio Padilla Airport is south of the town towards Tomarrazón and the main bus terminal is on Calle 15 (Avenida El Progreso)/Carrera 11.

Tourist information There is a tourist office, **Dirección de Turismo de Guajira** ① *C 1, Av de La Marina, No 4-42, T727 1015*, which has some information, but you may fnd more if you ask tour operators. Ask also for the University of the Guajira, which has an excellent resource centre related to the region and the Wayuú culture (ID is necessary to get in). The provincial website is www.laguajira.gov.co and the municipal site is www.riohacha-laguajira.gov.co.

Places in Riohacha
There are good white-sand beaches lined with coconut palms and a long wooden pier in the centre. Also two busy markets, the old market in town and a newer one further out, are worth a visit. At weekends Riohacha fills up, with bars and music springing up all over the place. The sea is clean, despite the dark silt stirred up by the waves and it is a good place to take stock before pushing through into the more remote areas of La Guajira.

Santuario Los Flamencos → *For listings, see pages 87-90.*

① *95 km east of Santa Marta and 25 km short of Riohacha. At the time of writing the Parques Nacionales Naturales de Colombia was not listing an entry fee for this park.*

The Santuario de Fauna y Flora Los Flamencos is 7000 ha of saline vegetation including mangroves and lagoons. There are several small, and two large, saline lagoons (Laguna Grande and Laguna de Navío Quebrado), separated from the Caribbean by sand bars. The latter is near **Camarones** (take a *colectivo* from the roundabout between the water tower and bus station in Riohacha, US$3), which is just off the main road. A road goes from Camarones to the park entrance at Guanebucane (3.5 km). The two large lagoons are fed by several intermittent streams which form deltas at the south point of the lakes and are noted for the many colonies of flamingos, some of which are there all year, others gather between November and May, during the wetter months when some fresh water enters the lagoons. The birds are believed to migrate to and from the Dutch Antilles, Venezuela and Florida. There is also plenty of other birdlife throughout the year.

At the northern end of **Laguna de Navío Quebrado** is a community-run visitor centre called **Los Mangles**, with accommodation in *cabañas*, in hammocks (**$**), or camping. Meals are also available and the centre arranges birdwatching trips on foot or by boat (US$5 per person). A two-day/one-night package costs US$73 based on two people sharing; longer packages are available. See www.ecoturismosantuario.weebly.com and www.parquesnacionales.gov.co. Beware that it gets very windy and sleeping in hammocks can be uncomfortable. Take plenty of water if walking. The locals survive, after the failure of the crustaceans in the lagoons, on tourism and ocean fishing. There are several bars/ restaurants and two shops on the beach.

Guajira Peninsula → *For listings, see pages 87-90.*

Beyond Riohacha to the east is the arid and sparsely inhabited Guajira Peninsula, with its magnificent sunsets. The indigenous peoples here, the Wayúu, collect *dividivi* (pods from a strangely wind-bent tree, the *Caesalpina coriaria*, which are mainly used for tanning), tend goats and fish. Look out for the coloured robes worn by the women. Increasingly, thanks to government schemes, they are now involved in tourism. The local language is Wayuunaiki; beyond Cabo de Vela little Spanish is spoken.

Arriving in the Guajira Peninsula
To visit the peninsula you can book a tour with one of the tour companies in Riohacha (see What to do, page 88). Alternatively, you can catch a ride in a *carrito*, a taxi shared with three others, on the paved road to Uribia (1½ hours, US$9) or Manaure (1¾ hours, US$10) and from there on dirt tracks to Cabo de la Vela (two to three hours). ►► *See Transport, page 89.*

Manaure and around
Manaure (www.manaure-laguajira.gov.co) is known for its salt flats southwest of the town. Hundreds of workers dig the salt and collect it in wheelbarrows, a bizarre sight against the glaring white background. If you walk along the beach for an hour, past the salt works, there are several lagoons where flamingos gather. Around 14 km from Manaure in this direction is **Musichi**, an important haunt of the flamingo, sometimes out of the wet season. It is an Area Natural Protegida de los Flamencos Rosados. Note that the birds may be on the other side of the lagoon and difficult to see; take binoculars. You can hire a moto-taxi or rent a bicycle in Manaure to go towards Musichi to see the flamingos. Take plenty of sunblock and water and a torch/flashlight for returning in the evening.

From Manaure there are early morning *busetas* to **Uribia** (30 minutes, US$3), and from there to Maicao, another hour. In Uribia, known as the indigenous capital of Colombia, you can buy authentic local handicrafts by asking around, but the town really doesn't have much to its name. It's also full of Venezuelan contraband and has a rough and ready feel to it. There is a **Wayúu Festival** here annually in June, www.festivalwayuu.com, at which *alijunas* (white people) are welcome, but ask permission before taking photographs. You can get *busetas* from Uribia to Puerto Bolívar (from where coal from El Cerrejón mine is exported) and from there transport to **Cabo de la Vela**. It costs about US$8 from Uribia to Cabo de Vela and the journey is slow as passengers are dropped off at their various *rancherías* (*busetas* run until 1400 but there are only a few on Sunday; all transport leaves from the market). The drive is spectacular with the final few kilometres involving a bumpy ride across a shimmering, dried-out salt lake that generates mirages. Cabo de la Vela is where the Wayúu believe their souls go after death, and is known as Jepirra. The barren landscape of shrubs and cacti only serves to accentuate the colour of the water, which glimmers in a dozen shades of aquamarine. In recent years tourism has really taken off and there are now more hostels in Cabo de la Vela than in Riohacha itself, all of them following the two-mile bay. There are various excursions from Cabo de la Vela, which include Pilón de Azúcar mountain, with lovely views of the sea, a nearby beach and also a lighthouse. The beach is beautiful and don't forget to look up at night for spectacular starry skies. To enjoy the deserted beaches, avoid Christmas and Easter when the *cabañas* and beaches are crowded and full of cars.

Getting to Cabo de la Vela independently is a time-consuming and at times uncomfortable experience, particularly during or immediately after, the wet season, although it can be done. It is far easier and recommended to book a tour from Riohacha, even though it will cost more than by public transport.

Macuira National Park
① *Entry US$18, Colombians US$6.20, children US$4. Registration and 30-min compulsory induction at Nazareth park office, guides US$20.*

Towards the northeast tip of the Guajira Peninsula is the Serranía de Macuira, named after the Makui people, ancestors of the Wayúu. The 25,000-ha park is entirely within the Wayúu reservation. It consists of a range of hills over 500 m, with microclimates of their own creating an oasis of tropical forest in the semi-desert. The highest point is **Cerro Palúa**, 865 m, and two other peaks are over 750 m. Moisture comes mainly from the northeast, which forms clouds in the evening that disperse in the early morning. The average temperature is 29°C and there is 450 mm of mist/rain providing water for the streams that disappear into the sand once they reach the plains. Macuira's remoteness has resulted in some interesting flora and fauna; notable wildlife includes the cardinal bird and 15 species of snake, including coral snakes. There are also Wayúu settlements little affected by outsiders, where the indigenous people cultivate cashew nuts, coconuts and plantains, as well as collecting dividivi pods. The rangers are all locals and are very friendly. A recommended walk in the park is a visit to the 40-m-high **El Chorro waterfall**, a delightful lush, green area.

Beyond Macuira is **Punta Gallinas**, the northernmost point in South America and a spectacular location. Nearby is **Taroa**, where sand dunes drop directly into the sea – perfect for a swim, but beware the waves are powerful here and the currents can be strong. Spending a few days exploring this area is a remarkable and rewarding experience. The landscape, usually arid and desolate, turns a bright shade of green after the rainy season and there are gorgeous bays for swimming and chilling. It's also the perfect place for getting closer to Wayúu culture and traditions.

Arriving in Macuira National Park To reach the Parque Natural Nacional Macuira you must travel northeast from Uribia along the mineral railway, then either round the coast past Bahía Portete, or direct across the semi-desert, to Nazareth on the east side of the park. There are no tourist facilities anywhere nearby and no public transport, though trucks may take you from the Bahía Portete area to **Nazareth** (seven to eight hours in the dry season), if you can find one. Nazareth is a Wayúu village where someone may let you stay the night in a hammock. Otherwise, there is camping beside the park office. It is recommended to take a local guide. The best way to visit is to contract your own jeep and guide. Beyond Cabo de la Vela we strongly advise you take a tour as there is no public transport, little Spanish is spoken and the locals aren't always welcoming. This is also a semi-self governing zone. **Aventure Colombia** in Cartagena (see page 42) arranges trips here from time to time. ▸▸ *See What to do, page 88.*

Note The Guajira Peninsula is not a place to travel alone, parties of three or more are recommended. If going in your own transport, check the situation before setting out. The roads can be in very bad condition, mostly dirt tracks and these can become impassable around the wet season. When the road is bad Punta Gallinas is only reached by boat from near Cabo de la Vela, two to three hours, often choppy and very wet. Also remember it is hot, it is easy to get lost, there is little mobile cover and very little water. Locals, including police, are very helpful in giving lifts.

Maicao
The paved Caribbean coastal highway continues from Riohacha inland to Maicao, 78 km, close to the Venezuelan border. Now that there are no flights from Barranquilla to Maracaibo, taxi or bus to Maicao and *colectivo* to Maracaibo is the most practical route. There is a new bus terminal to the east of town.

Maicao is hot, dusty and has a strong Arab presence, with several mosques and restaurants selling Arabic food. Clothing and white goods make up much of the business, but the city has a reputation for many black market activities. Most commercial premises close early and after dark the streets are unsafe.

East to Venezuela listings

For hotel and restaurant price codes and other relevant information, see pages 9-13.

⬤ Where to stay

Riohacha *p83, map p83*
$$$ Arimaca, C 1, No 8-75, T727 3481, www.hotelarimaca.com. Impressive high tower with clean, light and spacious rooms, some with reception room, all with balconies and magnificent sea views. There is a fine swimming pool on the 2nd floor, a good restaurant and buffet breakfast is included.
$$$ Majayura, Cra 10, No 1-40, T727 5242, majayurasol@hotmail.com.

Central hotel located near the beach. Restaurant, internet access, a/c, minibar and buffet breakfast included.
$$ Castillo del Mar, C 9A, No 15-352, T727 5043. Pleasant hotel by the sea, a bit rough around the edges, but very reasonably priced. Large rooms with a/c or fan. Recommended.
$ Almirante Padilla, Cra 6 y C 3a, T727 2328. Crumbling but with character, has an inviting patio and a restaurant with cheap *almuerzo*. It's clean, friendly, large and very central. Some rooms with a/c.
$ Internacional, Cra 7, No 13-37, T727 3483. Down an alleyway off the old market,

friendly with a pleasant restaurant on the patio. Free iced water. Recommended.
$ Yalconia del Mar, Cra 7, No 11-26, T727 3487. Private bath, cheaper with fan, clean, safe, friendly, helpful, halfway between the beach and the bus station.

Manaure and around *p85*
Manaure
$$ Palaaima, Cr 6, No 7-25, T717 8455/314-581 6789. Comfortable, cool rooms with a/c or fan, helpful. There are always Wayúu locals hanging around the hotel who are eager to talk about their culture and traditions.

Uribia
There are cheap, somewhat gotty options.
$ Hotel Juyasirain, C 14A 9-06, T717 7284. The only slightly more upmarket hotel in Uribia. Large, light and airy with a patio restaurant.

Cabo de la Vela
Along the coast, ask anyone and you will probably be able to get fried fish, coconut rice and a place to sling a hammock (US$7). There are now some 60 hostels along the beach, all offering roughly the same set-up for the same cost. Try **Playa Bonita**, in the main cluster of houses and shops, or **Pujurú**, further up the beach towards Pilón de Azúcar.

Punta Gallinas
$ Luz Mila. A lonely, but friendly little hostel and restaurant run by the Wayúu and where **Kai Ecotravel** (see below) has a base for their tours. Recommended.

Maicao *p87*
$$$-$$ Hotel Maicao Internacional, C 12, No 10-90, T726 7184. Good rooms with a/c, rooftop pool and bar. A good option in Maicao, attentive staff.
$$ Los Médanos, Cra 10, No 11-25, T726 8822. Large rooms, a bit dark, minibar, restaurant and disco.
$$ Maicao Plaza, C 10, No 10-28, T726 0310. Modern, central, with spacious rooms.

❼ Restaurants

Riohacha *p83, map p83*
Many ice cream and juice bars, and small *asados*, serving large, cheap selections of barbecued meat can be found at the western end of the seafront and there is also a row of picturesque, brightly painted huts serving ceviche and fresh seafood. The eastern end has more restaurants for sit-down meals.
$$ El Malecón, C 1, No 3-43. Good selection of seafood and meats served in a palm-thatched barn looking out to sea. There is music and dancing in the evenings. A good place for people-watching.
$$ La Tinaja, C 1, 4-59. Excellent seafood in light, breezy restaurant. Try the *Delicias de la casa* rice dish, tasty and substantial. Recommended.

✺ Festivals

Riohacha *p83, map p83*
Mar Festival Francisco el Hombre, www.festivalfranciscoelhombre.com. *Vallenato* festival.

❺ Shopping

Riohacha *p83, map p83*
Good hammocks sold in the market, 2 km from town on the road to Valledupar. The best place for buying local items is **La Casa de la Manta Guajira**, Cra 6 y C 12. Be prepared to bargain.

❹ What to do

Riohacha *p83, map p83*
Tour operators
Trips to the Guajira Peninsula are best arranged in Riohacha where there are several operators, but can also be taken with national operators and others in Cartagena and Santa Marta. Tours to Cabo de la Vela, 1-2 days, usually include Manaure (salt mines), Uribia, Pilón de Azucar and El Faro.

Hammocks

There's no better way to enjoy Colombia's beaches than to relax in a hammock, and there are abundant conveniently located palm trees to use as supports. Plenty of places hire them out but for true comfort it's best to buy your own.

The hammocks developed by the Wayúu are made up of intricately woven threads of cotton that form a crocheted net. These are known as *chinchorros* and they are larger than the average hammock, with wrap-around sides serving as a blanket and they often feature elaborate tassels. The other most common style uses brightly coloured woven cotton or wool to form a large stretch of material.

San Jacinto, a couple of hours south of Cartagena, is the capital of Colombia's hammock industry and the best place to find a bargain, but the market in Santa Marta also has a good selection. For *chinchorros*, the best places are the market in Riohacha and Uribia's handicraft shops in La Guajira.

All organize tours to Wayúu *rancherías* in the afternoon (includes a typical goat lunch).
Cabo de la Vela Turismo, T728 3684, www.cabodelavela.turismo.co. Runs tours throughout the region.
Comfaguajira, T728 2505, www.comfaguajira.com. Mon-Fri 0800-1200, 1400-1700.

Uribia
Kaí Ecotravel, Diagonal 1B, No 8-68, T717 7173, or T311-436 2830, also at Hotel Castillo del Mar in Riohacha and in Hotel Juyasirain, www.kaiecotravel.com (not working at time of writing, try kaiecotravel@turiscolombia.com). Run by a network of Wayúu families. Organizes tours to Cabo de la Vela (US$114 for 2 days), Parque Natural Nacional Macuira (US$454 for 4 days), Punta Gallinas (US$305 for 3 days), up to US$720 for an 8-day tour, all per person, including transport, accommodation and food.
Kaishi, T717 7306 or T311-429 6315, www.kaishitravel.com. Speak to Andrés Orozco, this company organizes jeep tours around La Guajira.

⊖ Transport

Riohacha *p83, map p83*
Early morning is best for travel; transport is scarce in the afternoon.

Air
There is 1 flight a day to **Bogotá**, 1 hr 35 mins, Avianca (C 7, No 7-04, T727 3624), where connections to other cities can be made.

Bus
It is best to travel from Riohacha in a luxury bus, in the early morning, as these are less likely to be stopped and searched for contraband. **Brasilia** runs Pullman buses to **Maicao**, frequent service, 1-1½ hrs, US$5.75.

Brasilia also has buses to **Santa Marta** (US$11, 3 hrs) and **Cartagena** US$24, every 30 mins. No direct buses to **Cabo de la Vela**: travel to **Uribia** and wait for a jeep (leaves when full). It's a long and uncomfortable journey. Some *colectivos* for Uribia and the northeast leave from the new market, 2 km southeast on the Valledupar road.

Taxi
Coopcaribe Taxis travel throughout the region and can be picked up almost anywhere in town, especially close to the old market area near the Hotel Internacional or outside Drogas La Rebaja. Daily to **Uribia**, 1½ hrs, US$9; **Manaure**, 1¾ hrs, US$10. They leave when full (4 people), be prepared to pay slightly more if there are no travellers.

Maicao *p87*
Bus
Brasilia has a frequent service to **Riohacha**,
US$5.75, as does **Copetrán**, US$5.15;
Santa Marta, 3 hrs, US$20; **Barranquilla**,
4-5 hrs, US$34 (also **Copetrán** US$18);
Cartagena, 6 hrs, US$34.

⊙ Directory

Riohacha *p83, map p83*
Banks Many are on or near Parque
Almirante Padilla. **Banco de Colombia**,
Cra 8, No 3-09, with ATMs. Also **Banco de
Bogotá**, Cra 7, No 1-38. **Embassies and
consulates** Venezuela, Cra 7, No 3-08,
p7-B, T727 4076, conve.corha@mppre.gob.
ve (Mon-Thu 0800-1200, 1400-1700, Fri 0800-
1300). If you need a visa, you should check
all requirements for your nationality before
arriving at this consulate. Travellers report it is
easier to get a Venezuelan visa in Barranquilla.
Immigration Migración Colombia, C 5,
No 4-48, 0800-1200, 1400-1700.

San Andrés and Providencia

San Andrés and Providencia are destinations most Colombians dream about visiting at least once in their lifetime. Closer to Nicaragua than to the Colombian mainland – there is a running dispute between the two countries over sovereignty – these Caribbean islands have what locals have dubbed 'the sea of seven colours', though it often seems like more. The waters around this archipelago play host to a variety of marine life, and the clarity of the sea makes this one of the best diving destinations in the Caribbean. In 2000, UNESCO declared the archipelago a World Biosphere Reserve, christened 'The Seaflower'. At 32 km in length, the Old McBean Lagoon barrier reef off Providencia is the third largest in the world.

Background

San Andrés and Providencia share a coastline rich in coral reefs, white-sand cays and waters of extraordinary colours, but are in fact very different. San Andrés, the larger island, is a popular mass tourism destination, replete with resort hotels and discos. Providencia has quietly observed its big sister's development, decided it does not want to follow the same path, and has put in place certain restrictions to halt the encroachment of package tourism.

The original inhabitants are mostly the descendants of Jamaican slaves brought over by English pirates such as Henry Morgan, and with the arrival of English, Dutch, French and Spanish settlers over the years this has led to an extraordinary genealogical mix. Today, especially in San Andrés, much of the original culture has been diluted and about 50% of the population is now made up of immigrants from mainland Colombia. The remainder are locals and there are Lebanese and Turkish communities too. Immigration is less pronounced in Providencia.

After Columbus spotted the islands on his fourth trip to the Caribbean, their early colonial history was dominated by the conflicts between Spain and England, though the Dutch occupied Providencia for some years. English Puritans arrived on Providencia from Bermuda and England in 1629 and later moved to San Andrés. The English left in 1641, but Creole English remained the dominant language until recent times and is still widely spoken. Surnames such as Whittaker, Hooker, Archbold, Robinson, Howard and Newell are also common. Providencia later became a pirate colony, shared between the Dutch and the English before it was taken back by the Spanish and assigned to the Vice Royalty of New Granada (modern-day Colombia) in 1803. In 1818 French Corsair Louis-Michel Aury successfully invaded Providencia and declared it part of the United States of Argentina and Chile, using it to capture Spanish cargo to bolster the burgeoning Latin American Independence movement. Finally, in 1822 San Andrés, Providencia and Santa Catalina were incorporated into the newly independent state of Gran Colombia.

The islands are 770 km north of continental Colombia, 849 km southwest of Jamaica, and 240 km east of Nicaragua. This proximity has led Nicaragua to claim them from Colombia in the past. Three battleships patrol San Andrés to guard against any invasion by the Nicaraguans.

San Andrés and around → *Phone code: 8. For listings, see pages 97-100.*

San Andrés, a coral island, is 11 km long, rising at its highest to 120 m. The town, commercial centre, major hotel sector and airport are at the northern end. A good view of the town can be seen from **El Cliff**. San Andrés is a popular, safe and local holiday destination for Colombians.

Arriving in San Andrés
Getting there A cheap way to visit San Andrés is by taking a charter flight from Bogotá or another major city for a weekend or a week, with accommodation and food included. Look for supplements in the Colombian newspapers and adverts on the internet.

1 San Andrés Island

Standards of hotel and restaurant packages can vary greatly. You may wish to opt for a cheap airfare and choose where to stay on arrival. The airport is 15 minutes' walk from town. Buses to the centre and San Luis go from across the road. A taxi is US$8.50, a *colectivo* US$1. Cruise ships and tours go to San Andrés but there are no other official passenger services by sea. ▶▶ *See Transport, page 100.*

Getting around Buses run every 15 minutes on the eastern side of the island, US$0.50, and more often at night and during the holidays. Taxis around the island cost US$20, but in town fares double after 2200.

Bicycles are easy to hire but are usually in poor condition, so choose your own bike and check all parts thoroughly. Motorbikes and golf buggies are also easy to hire.

Tourist information Staff at the **tourist office** ① *Av Newball, opposite Restaurante La Regatta, T512 5058, secturismosai@yahoo. com, Mon-Fri 0800-1200, 1400-1800, and kiosk at the end of Av 20 de Julio, across from the sea,* are helpful and English is spoken.

Where to stay 🛏
Casa Harb **1**
Sunset **2**

Restaurants 🍴
Bibi's Place **1**

> ➔ **San Andrés maps**
> 1 San Andrés Island, page 92
> 2 San Andrés town, page 94

They can also provide maps and hotel lists. The municipal website is www.sanandres.gov. co and the island's newspaper, the *San Andrés Hoy*, www.sanandreshoy.com, has some information in Spanish. On arrival in San Andrés, you must buy a tourist card, US$27, which is also valid for Providencia so don't lose it. You must also have an onward or return ticket.

Places on San Andrés

San Andrés and Providencia are famous in Colombia for their different styles of music, including the local form of calypso, soca, reggae and church music, as well as schottische, quadrille, polka and mazurka, the musical legacies of the various European communities that settled here. A number of good local groups perform on the islands and in Colombia. Look out for concerts at venues such as the **Old Coliseum** and the cultural centre at Punta Hansa in San Andrés town. There is also a **Museo Casa Isleña** ① *Av Circunvalar Km 5, 0900-1800, US$4.50*, a small historic house with displays relating to the culture of the island, including food, music and dance.

Besides the beautiful cays and beaches on the eastern side, see **Hoyo Soplador** (South End), a geyser-like hole through which the sea spouts into the air when the wind is in the right direction. The west coast is less spoilt, but there are no beaches on this side. Instead there is **El Cove** (The Cove), the island's deepest anchorage, and **Cueva de Morgan** (Morgan's Cave), reputed hiding place for pirate's treasure, which is penetrated by the sea through an underwater passage. Next to Cueva de Morgan is a **Pirate Museum** ① *entry US$5*, with exhibitions telling the history of the coconut, lots of paraphernalia salvaged from wrecks around the island and a replica pirate ship. About 1 km south from Cueva de Morgan is **West View** ① *daily 0900-1700*, an excellent place to see marine life as the sea is very clear. There is a small jetty with a diving board and slide and a small restaurant opposite the entrance.

At El Cove, you can continue round the coast, or cross the centre of the island back to town over **La Loma**. This is the highest point on the island and nearby is **La Laguna**, a freshwater lake 30 m deep, home to many birds and surrounded by palm and mango trees. On the town side of La Loma is the first **Baptist Church** to be built on the island (1847), acting as a beacon to shipping. The church has a Sunday service from 1000-1300 with gospel singing. If you take a turning just before the church you will reach the **Mirador Escalona**, a lookout point on someone's unfinished roof (US$1), from which there are spectacular views of the island. In the centre of the island you will find some life as it was before San Andrés became a tourist destination, with clapboard houses and traditional music.

Around San Andrés

Boats leave from San Andrés in the morning for El Acuario and Haynes Cay, and continue to Johnny Cay (frequently spelt Jhonny) in the afternoon, which has a white beach and parties all day Sunday (US$17 return). **El Acuario** (entry US$2.25) has crystalline water and is a good place to snorkel, and see eagle and manta rays. You can wade across the water to **Haynes Cay** where there is good food and a reggae bar at **Bibi's Place**. These are popular tours; if you want to avoid the crowds a good option is to hire a private boat (US$110 for the day) and do the tour in reverse. Boats for the cays leave from Tonino's Marina between 0930 and 1030, returning at 1530, or from Muelle Casa de la Cultura on Avenida Newell.

Apart from those already mentioned, other cays and islets in the archipelago are **Bolívar**, **Albuquerque**, **Algodón** (included in the Sunrise Park development in San Andrés), **Rocky**, the **Grunt**, **Serrana**, **Serranilla** and **Quitasueño**. On San Andrés the beaches are in town and on the eastern coast. Perhaps the best is at **San Luis** and **Bahía Sonora** (Sound Bay).

Diving
Diving off San Andrés is very good; the depth varies from 3-30 m, visibility from 30-60 m. There are three types of site: walls of seaweed and minor coral reefs, large groups of different types of coral, and underwater plateaux with much marine life. It is possible to dive in 70% of the insular platform. The **Pared Azul** (**Blue Wall**) is excellent for deep-water diving. **Black Coral Net** and **Morgan's Sponge** are other good sites. ▸▸ *See What to do, page 99.*

Providencia → *Phone code: 8. For listings, see pages 97-100.*

Providencia, also called **Old Providence**, 80 km to the north-northeast of San Andrés, is 7 km long and 3.5 km wide. The island is more mountainous and considerably more verdant than San Andrés, rising to 360 m, due to its volcanic origin and is much older. There are waterfalls, and the land drops steeply into the sea in places.

Providencia is striving to retain its cultural identity. Hotels must be constructed in the typical clapboard style of the island and cannot be built higher than two storeys, while mainland operators cannot manage them directly; they must work in partnership with local owners. Only locals are allowed to buy property on the island and outsiders can stay no longer than six months at a time.

Arriving on Providencia
Getting there Visitors can arrive by air from San Andrés (20 minutes) or by sea on launches and boats that ferry goods over to Providencia. Beware that the sea can be choppy on this trip. ▸▸ *See Transport, page 100.*

Getting around *Chivas* (brightly coloured buses) circle the island at more or less regular intervals, the standard fare is US$2. *Colectivos* can also be found on the island and charge much the same.

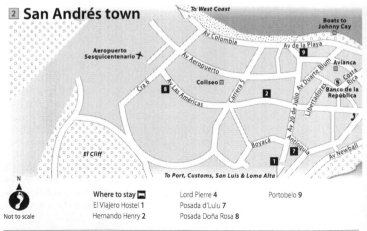

2 San Andrés town

Where to stay 🛏
El Viajero Hostel 1
Hernando Henry 2

Lord Pierre 4
Posada d'Lulu 7
Posada Doña Rosa 8

Portobelo 9

Not to scale

The black crabs of Providencia

With the arrival of the first rains between April and June, Providencia is the scene of a spectacular natural phenomenon. Each night during the wet season thousands of black crabs (*Gecarcinus lateralis*) descend from the forests of High Hill and release their eggs in the waters between South West Bay and Freshwater, wriggling their abdomens in the surf to deposit their eggs. The hatchlings are born in the sea and return to the hills one month later.

During the migration the road that encircles the island is closed to traffic, thus allowing the crabs free access to the beaches without the risk of being run over. **Coralina** (www.coralina.gov.co), the government's environmental agency on the archipelago, has banned the capture and eating of crabs during the breeding season and anyone caught disobeying the ban risks a heavy fine equivalent to three months of the minimum wage.

Many of the islanders make a living from crab fishing but during this time hunters turn protectors as they are employed as enforcers of the ban, thus ensuring that Providencia's black crab population will continue to thrive.

Tourist office In the **Centro Administrativo Aury** ① *T514 8054, securismoprovidencia@hotmail.com*.

Around the island

Day tours are arranged through hotels around the island, stopping typically at Cayo Cangrejo to swim and snorkel (entry US$1.50). Snorkelling equipment can be hired and diving trips arranged: the best places are Aguadulce and South West Bay.

In 1996 part of the east coast and offshore reefs and coral islands were declared a national park (**Parque Nacional Natural Old Providence – McBean Lagoon**, entry US$7 for non-nationals). The land position includes Iron Wood Hill (150 m), mainly small trees but including cockspur (*Acacia colinsii*) which has large conical-shaped needles, home to a species of ant (*Pseudo-myrmex ferruginea*) with a very painful sting. There are superb views from **Casabaja** (Bottom House) or **Aguamansa** (Smooth Water), a climb to the summit will take about one hour, and with a guide will cost US$15. You will see relics of the fortifications built on the island during its disputed ownership.

➡ San Andrés maps
1 San Andrés Island, page 92
2 San Andrés town, page 94

Restaurants ⑦ Niko's **3**
Club Náutico & La Regatta **1**
Margherita e Carbonara **2**

Horse riding is available, and boat trips can be made to neighbouring islands such as **Santa Catalina**, an old pirate lair separated from Providencia by a channel cut for their better defence. To the northeast is **Cayo Cangrejo** (Crab Cay), a beautiful place for swimming and snorkelling, and **Cayos Tres Hermanos** (Three Brothers Cays). Boat trips leave from 1000-1500, with a two-hour lunch in South West Bay. Santa Catalina is joined to the main island by a 100-m wooden bridge, known as the

Puente de los Amantes (Lovers' Bridge). On the west side of Santa Catalina are the ruins of an old fort, built by the English to defend their pirate colony. Formerly known as Fort Warwick, it was rechristened **Fuerte de la Libertad** after the island was retaken by the Spanish in the 17th century. The fort still has the original canons and it is rumoured that there is a secret cave which was used by Henry Morgan to escape to the sea below (most probably untrue). Beyond the fort is a fine beach, excellent for snorkelling, with caves with air chambers and lots of starfish. Further still is a rock formation called **Morgan's Head**; seen from the side it looks like a man's profile. The path beyond Morgan's Head leads through thick forest to the top of the mountain and an abandoned house formerly belonging to a drug trafficker.

Providencia

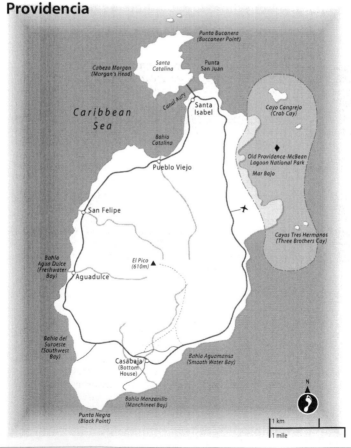

The beaches
Bahía Manzanillo (Manchineel Bay) is named after the manzanillo trees found on its edges (the fruit is like a miniature apple, sweet smelling but with an acid taste – and dangerous; do not eat), and is the largest, most attractive and least developed, with a couple of restaurants, including **Roland's Roots Bar** (see page 99). **Bahía del Suroeste** (South West Bay) is fringed by almond trees, palms and has bottle green water, and on Saturday afternoons the local boys put on bareback horse races. **Bahía Agua Dulce** (Freshwater Bay) has a small strip of beach and the sea laps at the fronts of the many hotels in this small bay. Two smaller beaches are **Alan's Bay**, between Aguadulce and San Felipe, which is very secluded and seldom visited, and **Playa del Fuerte**, underneath the fort on Santa Catalina, which has excellent snorkelling and lots of starfish.

San Andrés and Providencia listings

For hotel and restaurant price codes and other relevant information, see pages 9-13.

◎ Where to stay

San Andrés *p92, maps p92 and p94*
Hotels quote rates per person, but we list prices for double rooms. Prices include half board, but most can be booked without meals. Most raise prices by 20-30% on 15 Dec. This also applies to Providencia. The **Decameron** group has 5 hotels on San Andrés, www.decameron.com.
$$$$ Casa Harb, C 11, No 10-83, La Rocosa, T512 6348, www.casaharb.com. Just outside town, this boutique hotel takes its inspiration from the Far East and is the most stylish location on the island. Each room is individually decorated with antique furniture. The baths, made of solid granite, are enormous. A former family home, this mansion has a an infinity pool and offers home-cooked meals.
$$$$ Lord Pierre, Av Colombia, No 1B-106, T512 7541, www.lordpierre.com. It boasts a magnificent pier on the tip of the *malecón*, but some of the services are a bit dated. Rooms are large with heavy furniture.
$$$ Portobelo, Av Colombia, No 5A-69, T512 7008, www.portobelohotel.com. Occupies a couple of buildings on western end of the *malecón*. Rooms have large beds, a/c and cable TV. Breakfast included. (**$$$$** in high season).

$$$ Sunset Hotel, Carretera Circunvalar Km 13, T513 0433, sunsetsai@hotmail.com. On the western side of the island, this is the perfect place to stay if you want to do some serious diving – or just want to escape the crowds. It has bright, fresh rooms with high ceilings, all set around a saltwater swimming pool. With a restaurant serving a mixture of international and regional food in a typical clapboard house and a dive shop next door, this is one of the best places to unwind in San Andrés.
$$ Hernando Henry, Av Las Américas, No 4-84, T512 3416, anggyhenry@ hotmail.com. At the back of town, this hotel has shoddy but passable rooms. TV and laundry service. Rooms are significantly cheaper with fan.
$$ La Posada D'Lulú, Av Antioquia, No 2-28, T512 2919. This brightly coloured hostel with its clean and comfortable rooms is one of the best mid-range options in town. There are 2 apartments to rent for longer stays and an excellent restaurant serving home cooked food for US$3. Recommended.
$$ Posada Doña Rosa, Av Las Américas con Aeropuerto, T512 3649, www.posada rosa.blogspot.com. A 2-min walk from the airport, this is a reasonable and economical option. It has clean rooms with private bathrooms and a small patio with potted plants. There is a kitchen and TV room, and it's a short walk from the beach. Also has 2 apartments to rent.

$$-$ pp El Viajero Hostel, Av 20 de Julio
No 3A-122, T512 7497, www.elviajerohostels.
com/hostel-san-andres. A member of the
Uruguayan hostel chain. It has private
rooms and dorms (US$17-26 per bed),
with breakfast included in the price, bicycles
can be hired and money can be exchange.

Providencia *p94, map p96*
Rooms can be rented at affordable prices
in local houses or *posadas nativas*.

Hotels in Agua Dulce are 10 mins by
motor taxi (US$1) from the centre or a 1-hr
walk. Suroeste is a 20-min walk from Agua
Dulce. The Decameron group, www.
decameron.com, represents 5 properties
on the island, including **Cabañas Miss Elma**,
T514 8229, and **Cabañas Miss Mary**, T514
8454, at Aguadulce.
$$$$ Deep Blue Hotel, Maracaibo Bay,
T321-458 2099, www.hoteldeepblue.com.
Luxury 'boutique' hotel set in tropical forest.
It offers splendid views of Crab Caye and
the Caribbean. There's a tapas restaurant by
the sea and visitors get complimentary use
of the hotel's sea kayaks. It has an infinity
pool and staff can arrange scuba diving and
other excursions. Good sustainability and
environmental policies. Recommended.
$$$ Posada del Mar, Aguadulce, T514
8168, posadadelmar@latinmail.com
(www. decameron.com). Pink and purple
clapboard house with comfortable rooms,
each with a terrace and hammock looking
onto the bay. The sea laps at the edge of
the garden. Has cable TV, a/c, minibar and
hot water. Recommended.
$$$ Sirius, South West Bay, T514 8213,
www.siriushotel.net. Large, colourful house
set back from the beach, run by a Swiss
family. The rooms are large and light, some
have balconies with hammocks. Kitchen
available for guests. Also dive centre, kayaks,
wakeboarding, horse riding, massage. The
owner speaks German, Italian and English.
Half-board and diving packages available.
$$$ Sol Caribe Providencia, Agua Dulce,
T514 8230, www.solarhoteles.com. Chain

hotel offering 2- to 5-night packages, pool,
sea views, a/c, TV, fridge, bright.
$$ Hotel Old Providence, diagonal
Alcaldía Municipal, Santa Isabel, T514 8691.
Above supermarket Erika, rooms are basic
but clean and have a/c, cable TV, fridge and
private bathroom.

🍴 Restaurants

San Andrés *p92, maps p92 and p94*
$$$-$$ La Regatta, Av Newball, next to
Club Náutico, T512 0437. Seafood restaurant
on a pier, fine reputation.
$$$-$$ Margherita e Carbonara,
Av Colombia, No 1-93, opposite the
Lord Pierre Hotel. Italian-owned restaurant
decorated with photographs from Italian
films. Good pizzas.
$$ Bibi's Place, Haynes Caye, T513 3767,
caritoortega@hotmail.com. Reggae bar
and restaurant on cay next to El Acuario
serving seafood, including crab and lobster.
Organizes full moon parties and civil and
rasta weddings.
$$ Niko's, Av Colombia, No 1-93. Bills itself
as a seafood restaurant though its steaks are
actually better. Lovely setting by the water.

Providencia *p94, map p96*
Local specialities include crab soup and
rondón, a mix of fish, conch, yucca and
dumplings, cooked in coconut milk. Corn
ice cream is also popular – it tastes a
little like vanilla but sweeter. Breadfruit, a
grapefruit-sized fruit with a taste similar
to potato, is the archipelago's official fruit.

As well as hotel restaurants, good places
include: **Arturo**, on Suroeste beach, next to
Miss Mary. **Café Studio**, between Agua Dulce
and Suroeste. Great pies and spaghetti.
$$ Caribbean Place (Donde Martín),
Aguadulce. *Bogoteño* chef Martín Quintero
arrived for a brief stay in 1989 and has never
left. He uses local ingredients. Specialities
include lobster in crab sauce, fillet of fish
in ginger and corn ice cream.

$$ Roland's Roots Bar, Playa Manzanillo, T514 8417, rolandsbeach@hotmail.com. Roland is a legend on the island, as are the parties at his bar-restaurant on Manzanillo Beach. The menu is mainly seafood, with fried fish and ceviches.

🎉 Festivals

San Andrés *p92, maps p92 and p94*
Apr Festival del Cangrejo. Celebrating the crab and all the many ways it can be prepared to eat, plus music and dancing.
20 Jul Independence, which incorporates a Festival del Mar.
Late Oct Green Moon Festival. A popular music festival which has been revived after several years' absence.
End-Nov Reinado del Coco. The crowning of the Coconut Queen coinciding with the festival of the island's patron saint.

Providencia *p94, map p96*
Jun Carnival.

🛒 Shopping

Providencia *p94, map p96*
Arts and Crafts Café, Aqua Dulce, T514 8297. French owners sell local crafts and delicious home-made cookies and ice-cream.

🎯 What to do

San Andrés *p92, maps p92 and p94*
Canopying
Canopy La Loma, Vía La Loma-Barrack, T314-447 9868. Has a site at the top of the hill in San Andrés. 3 'flights' over the trees (450 m, 300 m and 200 m above sea level) with spectacular views out to sea. Good safety precautions and equipment.

Diving
Banda Dive Shop, Hotel Lord Pierre, Local 102, T315-303 5428, www.bandadiveshop. com. PADI qualified, offers various courses. Fast boat and good equipment.

Sharky Dive Shop, Carretera Circunvalar Km 13, T512 0651, www.sharkydiveshop.com. Next to **Sunset Hotel**, Sharky's has good equipment and excellent, English-speaking guides. PADI qualifications and a beginners' course held in the Sunset's saltwater pool.

Watersports and boat trips
From Toninos Marina there are boat trips to the nearby cays, US$17 with lunch included.
Cooperativa Lancheros, on the beach in San Andrés town. Can arrange fishing trips, windsurfing, jet skiing and kitesurfing. Snorkelling equipment can be hired for US$10.
Galeón Morgan, Centro Comercial New Point Plaza, T512 8787. Boat tours to El Acuario.

Providencia *p94, map p96*
Diving
Recommended diving spots on the Old McBean Lagoon reef are **Manta's Place**, a good place to see manta rays; **Felipe's Place** where there is a submerged figure of Christ; and **Stairway to Heaven**, which has a large wall of coral and big fish.
Felipe Diving, South West Bay, T851 8775, www.felipediving.com. Mini and full courses, also rents snorkel equipment, can arrange lodging. Owner Felipe Cabeza even has a diving spot on the reef named after him. Warmly recommended. See also **Hotel Sirius**, above. PADI qualifications.

Snorkelling and boat trips
Recommended snorkelling sites include the waters around Santa Catalina, where there are many caves to explore as well as **Morgan's Head** and lots of starfish; **Hippie's Place**, which has a little bit of everything; and **El Faro** (The Lighthouse), the end of the reef before it drops into deep sea, some 14 km from Providencia.
Valentina Tours, T514 8548. Lemus Walter, aka Captain 'Hippie', organizes snorkelling, and boat trips to the outlying cays and reefs. He has a section of the reef named after him. He charges US$140 for a day's hire of the boat.

Tour operators

Body Contact, Aguadulce, T514 8283. Owner Jennifer Archbold organizes excursions, fishing and hiking trips, currency exchange, accommodation, and more. Recommended.

Walking

There is a good walk over Manchineel Hill, between Bottom House (Casa Baja) and South West Bay, 1.5 km through tropical forest, with fine views of the sea; many types of bird can be seen, along with iguanas and blue lizards. Guided tours depart twice a day at 0900 and 1500 from Bottom House. Enquire at **Body Contact**, see Tour operators, above, or **Coralina**, T514 9003.

⊖ Transport

San Andrés *p92, maps p92 and p94*
Air
Flights to **Bogotá**, **Cali**, **Medellín** and **Cartagena** with AeroRepública; Avianca, Av Colón, Edif Onaissi local 107, T512 3212, airport T512 3213; Satena, T512 1403 San Andrés, T514 9257 Providencia; and **Searca** (booked through Decameron). Copa (Av Newball, No 4-141, Torre Sunrise Beach, local 125-B6) has a flight daily to **Panama City**. To **Providencia** 2 times a day with **Satena** and **Searca**. Bookable only in San Andrés. It is essential to confirm flights to guarantee a seat. Schedules change frequently.

Boat

Catamaran *Sensation*, www.catamaranel sensation.com, sails Mon, Wed, Fri, Sun 0730, from San Andrés to **Providencia**, returning at 1530, US$74 one way, 3¼ hrs. Cargo boat trips leave from San Andrés, taking 7-8 uncomfortable hrs, 3 times a week, US$22. They usually leave at 2200, arriving in the early morning. *Miss Isabel*, *Doña Olga* and *Raziman* make the trip regularly. Speak directly to the captain at the port in San Andrés, or enquire at the Port Authority (*Capitanía del Puerto*) in San Luis.

Vehicle and bicycle hire

Motorbikes are easy to hire, US$35 per day, as are golf buggies, US$83 per day. Cars can be hired for 2 hrs or for the day. Passport may be required as deposit.

Bikes are a popular way of getting around on the island and are easy to hire, too, but they may be in poor condition.

Providencia *p94, map p96*
Vehicle and bicycle hire

Mopeds can be hired for US$35 per day from many of the hotels and golf buggies are also available for US$83 per day.

⊙ Directory

San Andrés *p92, maps p92 and p94*
Banks Banks close 1200-1400. ATMs available in town and at the airport. *Casa de cambio*, some shops and most hotels will change US$ cash. **Immigration** Migración Colombia, Cra 7, No 2-70, T512 1818.

Providencia *p94, map p96*
Banks An ATM is tucked away just before the Lover's Bridge, on the road to Santa Catalina. **Useful numbers** Police: T2. Medical: T11. Ambulance: T514 8016 at hospital.

Contents

Footnotes

Index

Titles available in the Footprint *Focus* range

Latin America	UK RRP	US RRP
Bahia & Salvador	£7.99	$11.95
Brazilian Amazon	£7.99	$11.95
Brazilian Pantanal	£6.99	$9.95
Buenos Aires & Pampas	£7.99	$11.95
Cartagena & Caribbean Coast	£7.99	$11.95
Costa Rica	£8.99	$12.95
Cuzco, La Paz & Lake Titicaca	£8.99	$12.95
El Salvador	£5.99	$8.95
Guadalajara & Pacific Coast	£6.99	$9.95
Guatemala	£8.99	$12.95
Guyana, Guyane & Suriname	£5.99	$8.95
Havana	£6.99	$9.95
Honduras	£7.99	$11.95
Nicaragua	£7.99	$11.95
Northeast Argentina & Uruguay	£8.99	$12.95
Paraguay	£5.99	$8.95
Quito & Galápagos Islands	£7.99	$11.95
Recife & Northeast Brazil	£7.99	$11.95
Rio de Janeiro	£8.99	$12.95
São Paulo	£5.99	$8.95
Uruguay	£6.99	$9.95
Venezuela	£8.99	$12.95
Yucatán Peninsula	£6.99	$9.95

Asia	UK RRP	US RRP
Angkor Wat	£5.99	$8.95
Bali & Lombok	£8.99	$12.95
Chennai & Tamil Nadu	£8.99	$12.95
Chiang Mai & Northern Thailand	£7.99	$11.95
Goa	£6.99	$9.95
Gulf of Thailand	£8.99	$12.95
Hanoi & Northern Vietnam	£8.99	$12.95
Ho Chi Minh City & Mekong Delta	£7.99	$11.95
Java	£7.99	$11.95
Kerala	£7.99	$11.95
Kolkata & West Bengal	£5.99	$8.95
Mumbai & Gujarat	£8.99	$12.95

Africa & Middle East	UK RRP	US RRP
Beirut	£6.99	$9.95
Cairo & Nile Delta	£8.99	$12.95
Damascus	£5.99	$8.95
Durban & KwaZulu Natal	£8.99	$12.95
Fès & Northern Morocco	£8.99	$12.95
Jerusalem	£8.99	$12.95
Johannesburg & Kruger National Park	£7.99	$11.95
Kenya's Beaches	£8.99	$12.95
Kilimanjaro & Northern Tanzania	£8.99	$12.95
Luxor to Aswan	£8.99	$12.95
Nairobi & Rift Valley	£7.99	$11.95
Red Sea & Sinai	£7.99	$11.95
Zanzibar & Pemba	£7.99	$11.95

Europe	UK RRP	US RRP
Bilbao & Basque Region	£6.99	$9.95
Brittany West Coast	£7.99	$11.95
Cádiz & Costa de la Luz	£6.99	$9.95
Granada & Sierra Nevada	£6.99	$9.95
Languedoc: Carcassonne to Montpellier	£7.99	$11.95
Málaga	£5.99	$8.95
Marseille & Western Provence	£7.99	$11.95
Orkney & Shetland Islands	£5.99	$8.95
Santander & Picos de Europa	£7.99	$11.95
Sardinia: Alghero & the North	£7.99	$11.95
Sardinia: Cagliari & the South	£7.99	$11.95
Seville	£5.99	$8.95
Sicily: Palermo & the Northwest	£7.99	$11.95
Sicily: Catania & the Southeast	£7.99	$11.95
Siena & Southern Tuscany	£7.99	$11.95
Sorrento, Capri & Amalfi Coast	£6.99	$9.95
Skye & Outer Hebrides	£6.99	$9.95
Verona & Lake Garda	£7.99	$11.95

North America	UK RRP	US RRP
Vancouver & Rockies	£8.99	$12.95

Australasia	UK RRP	US RRP
Brisbane & Queensland	£8.99	$12.95
Perth	£7.99	$11.95

For the latest books, e-books and a wealth of travel information, visit us at: www.footprinttravelguides.com.

footprint travelguides.com

Join us on facebook for the latest travel news, product releases, offers and amazing competitions: www.facebook.com/footprintbooks.

11/15

CUNARD

THE MOST FAMOUS OCEAN LINERS IN THE WORLD™

24 Hour Loan Only

Credits

Footprint credits

Editor: Nicola Gibbs
Production and layout: Emma Bryers
Maps and cover: Kevin Feeney

Publisher: Patrick Dawson
Managing Editor: Felicity Laughton
Advertising: Elizabeth Taylor
Sales and marketing: Kirsty Holmes

Photography credits

Front cover: Javarman/Dreamstime.com
Back cover: Shutterstock/Jess Kraft

Printed in Great Britain by 4edge Limited,
Hockley, Essex

Every effort has been made to ensure that
the facts in this guidebook are accurate.
However, travellers should still obtain advice
from consulates, airlines, etc, about travel
and visa requirements before travelling.
The authors and publishers cannot accept
responsibility for any loss, injury or
inconvenience however caused.

Publishing information

Footprint *Focus Cartagena & Caribbean Coast*
2nd edition
© Footprint Handbooks Ltd
October 2013

ISBN: 978 1 909268 38 8
CIP DATA: A catalogue record for this book
is available from the British Library

® Footprint Handbooks and the Footprint
mark are a registered trademark of
Footprint Handbooks Ltd

Published by Footprint
6 Riverside Court
Lower Bristol Road
Bath BA2 3DZ, UK
T +44 (0)1225 469141
F +44 (0)1225 469461
footprinttravelguides.com

Distributed in the USA by Globe Pequot
Press, Guilford, Connecticut